Table of Contents

Block of the Month Sampler Quilt

Christmas Goodies

When I first started quilting, I deeply admired vintage sampler quilts, but definitely from a safe distance. They looked way too involved and complicated for me to tackle, until one day I decided to dive in and created one as a block of the month program. I have been completely smitten with them ever since! There is something so freeing about dividing the project into a monthly block assignment with the knowledge that if I keep up, I will have one of those wonderful samplers by the end of the year.

This Christmas Figs Block of the Month Quilt is one of those samplers – drawn from the richness of historical samplers. Years ago, I designed and offered this as a limited block of the month program. Now I am so glad to release the patterns for the first time in this book for everyone to enjoy. Christmas at our house is red, green and cream through and through and I am thrilled to keep this traditional feel with my Christmas Figs collection for Moda Fabrics.

I hope you join me on this journey and enjoy each month as much as I have. If you find that you have fallen in love with one of the monthly blocks, you also have 10 coordinating projects to choose from in addition to the sampler! These have been lovingly stitched by some of my best quilting friends and we are so happy to share them with you here.

Happy Stitching, Joanna Figueroa

Block of the Month Sampler Quilt Fabric Requirements

Use ¼" seams and press as arrows indicate throughout.

78 ½" x 96 ½"

Month One

| Ivory Tonal 20318-14 ½ yard | Red Tonal 20318-11 14" x 21" | Olive Star Dot 20312-13 10" x 21" | Ivory Gingham 20313-14 ⅓ yard | Olive/Ivory Star Dot 20312-22 10" x 21" | Red Scallop 20315-11 15" x 21" | Green Star Dot 20312-12 10" x 21" |

Month Two

| Olive/Ivory Star Dot 20312-22 ⅓ yard | Red Star Dot 20312-11 12" x 21" | Green Scallop 20315-12 14" x 21" | Ivory Tonal 20318-14 ½ yard | Red Gingham 20313-11 15" x 21" | Olive Star Dot 20312-13 15" x 21" |

Month Three

| Ivory Tonal 20318-14 ⅓ yard | Ivory Gingham 20313-14 ⅝ yard | Red Gingham 20313-11 10" x 21" | Red Tonal 20318-11 10" x 21" | Red Star Dot 20312-11 10" x 21" | Green Scallop 20315-12 10" x 21" | Olive Garland 20317-13 10" x 21" |
| Red/Ivory Star Dot 20312-21 11" x 21" | Green Tiles 20316-12 16" x 21" | | | | | |

Month Four

| Ivory Gingham 20313-14 ½ yard | Red Star Dot 20312-11 11" x 21" | Red Garland 20317-11 10" x 21" | Green Gingham 20313-12 22" x 21" | Ivory Tonal 20318-14 13" x 21" | Red/Ivory Star Dot 20312-21 10" x 21" | Olive/Ivory Star Dot 20312-22 10" x 21" |
| Red Tiles 20316-11 14" x 21" | Red Tonal 20318-11 10" x 21" | ½" Bias Tape Maker | Applique Glue | | | |

Month Five

Ivory Gingham 20313-14 18" x 21"	Olive/Ivory Star Dot 20312-22 10" x 21"	Red Star Dot 20312-11 10" x 21"	Red Scallop 20315-11 14" x 21"	Green Tiles 20316-12 10" x 21"	Olive Garland 20317-13 10" x 21"	Ivory Tonal 20318-14 10" x 21"
Ivory Star Dot 20312-14 10" x 21"	Red/Ivory Star Dot 20312-21 10" x 21"	Green Star Dot 20312-12 13" x 21"				

Month Six

Olive/Ivory Star Dot 20312-22 16" x 21"	Berry Scallop 20315-14 13" x 21"	Green Scallop 20315-12 10" x 10"	Green Gingham 20313-12 10" x 10"	Olive Gingham 20313-22 10" x 10"	Olive Star Dot 20312-13 10" x 10"	Green Tiles 20316-12 10" x 10"
Green Star Dot 20312-12 10" x 10"	Ivory Tonal 20318-14 13" x 21"	Red/Ivory Star Dot 20312-21 12" x 21"	Red Gingham 20313-11 13" x 21"	Olive Garland 20317-13 10" x 21"		

Month Seven

Ivory Gingham 20313-14 ⅝ yard	Red Garland 20317-11 14" x 21"	Olive Star Dot 20312-13 13" x 21"	Red/Ivory Star Dot 20312-21 10" x 10"	Ivory Star Dot 20312-14 10" x 10"	Red Gingham 20313-11 11" x 21"	Red Tiles 20316-11 10" x 21"
Green Scallop 20315-12 10" x 21"						

Block of the Month Sampler Quilt Fabric Requirements

Month Eight

Ivory Tonal 20318-14 22" x 21"	Red/Ivory Star Dot 20312-21 10" x 21"	Ivory Gingham 20313-14 10" x 21"	Ivory Star Dot 20312-14 16" x 21"	Red Scallop 20315-11 10" x 21"	Berry Gingham 20313-21 10" x 21"	Red Star Dot 20312-11 10" x 21"
Red Tiles 20316-11 10" x 21"	Green Tiles 20316-12 10" x 21"	Green Star Dot 20312-12 10" x 21"	Olive Gingham 20313-22 10" x 21"	Green Scallop 20315-12 15" x 21"	Red Gingham 20313-11 13" x 21"	

Month Nine

Ivory Tonal 20318-14 ⅝ yard	Ivory Star Dot 20312-14 10" x 21"	Ivory Gingham 20313-14 10" x 21"	Olive/Ivory Star Dot 20312-22 10" x 21"	Berry Gingham 20313-21 10" x 21"	Red Tiles 20316-11 10" x 21"	Olive Star Dot 20312-13 10" x 21"
Green Scallop 20315-12 10" x 21"	Red/Ivory Star Dot 20312-21 10" x 21"	Red Gingham 20313-11 ¼ yard	Green Star Dot 20312-12 10" x 10"	Green Gingham 20313-12 10" x 10"		

Month Ten

Ivory Tonal 20318-14 10" x 21"	Ivory Gingham 20313-14 21" x 21"	Olive/Ivory Star Dot 20312-22 14" x 21"	Red Star Dot 20312-11 18" x 21"	Red Tonal 20318-11 16" x 21"	Red/Ivory Star Dot 20312-21 12" x 21"	Red Scallop 20315-11 13" x 21"
Green Tiles 20316-12 10" x 21"	Olive Garland 20317-13 13" x 21"					

Month Eleven

Red Star Dot
20312-11
12" x 21"

Olive Gingham
20313-22
12" x 21"

Month Twelve

Ivory Tonal
20318-14
2 ¾ yards

Berry Gingham
20313-21
⅞ yard

Backing

Ivory Holly
20310-14
7 ⅜ yards

Longarm quilter
Karolyn Nubin Jensen

Month One – Puzzle Star Block

Unfinished size: 16 ½" x 16 ½"
Make one

Cutting Instructions

Ivory Tonal
2 - 3" x 42" strips, subcut into:
   18 - 3" squares   A

2 - 1 ⅜" x 42" strips, subcut into:
   2 - 1 ⅜" x 16 ½" rectangles   B
   2 - 1 ⅜" x 14 ¾" rectangles   C

2 - 1 ¼" x 42" strips, subcut into:
   20 - 1 ¼" x 2 ½" rectangles   D
   4 - 1 ¼" squares   E

Red Tonal
2 - 3" x 21" strips, subcut into:
   12 - 3" squares   F

3 - 1 ¼" x 21" strips, subcut into:
   16 - 1 ¼" x 2 ½" rectangles   G
   4 - 1 ¼" squares   H

Olive Star Dot
1 - 3" x 21" strip, subcut into:
   6 - 3" squares   I
   From remainder of strip cut:
   1 - 1 ¼" square   J

Block Instructions

Cut on the diagonal once.

Make thirty-six.

Make twenty-four.

Make twelve.

Assemble Unit.

Trim Red Half Square Triangle Unit to measure 2 ½" x 2 ½".

Make twenty-four.

Assemble Unit.

Trim Green Half Square Triangle Unit to measure 2 ½" x 2 ½".

Make twelve.

Assemble Unit.

Corner Unit should measure 5 ¼" x 5 ¼".

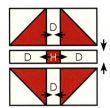 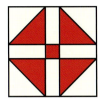

Make four.

Assemble Unit.

Middle Unit should measure 5 ¼" x 5 ¼".

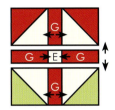 

Make four.

Assemble Unit.

Center Unit should measure 5 ¼" x 5 ¼".

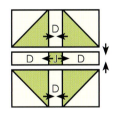 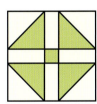

Make one.

Assemble Unit.

Puzzle Star Unit should measure 14 ¾" x 14 ¾".

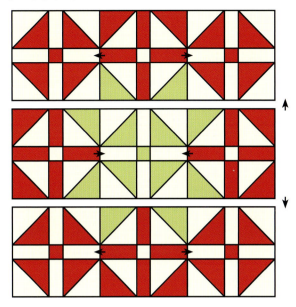

Make one.

Assemble Block.

Puzzle Star Block should measure 16 ½" x 16 ½".

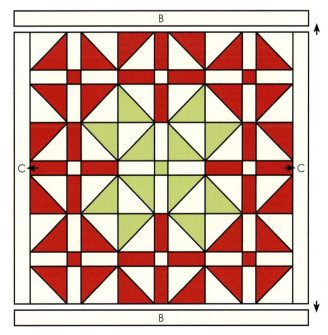

Make one.

Month One - Pineapple Block

Unfinished size: 16 ½" x 16 ½"
Make one

Cutting Instructions

Ivory Tonal
2 - 1" x 42" strips, subcut into:
2 - 1" x 16 ½" rectangles	A
2 - 1" x 15 ½" rectangles	B

Ivory Gingham
4 - 2" x 42" strips, subcut into:
2 - 2" x 15 ½" rectangles	C
4 - 2" x 12 ½" rectangles	D
4 - 2" x 9 ½" rectangles	E
2 - 2" x 6 ½" rectangles	F

Olive/Ivory Star Dot
1 - 2" x 21" strip, subcut into:
2 - 2" x 6 ½" rectangles	G
2 - 2" x 3 ½" rectangles	H

Red Scallop
3 - 3 ½" x 21" strips, subcut into:
12 - 3 ½" squares	I

Green Star Dot
1 - 3 ½" x 21" strip, subcut into:
4 - 3 ½" squares	J
1 - 3 ½" square	K

Block Instructions

Scallop print can be sewn all one direction or scrappy.

Assemble Unit.

Partial Center Unit should measure 6 ½" x 6 ½".

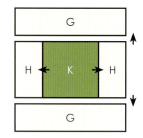 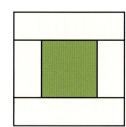

Make one.

Draw a diagonal line on the wrong side of the Fabric J squares.

With right sides facing, layer a Fabric J square on one corner of the Partial Center Unit.

Stitch on the drawn line and trim ¼" away from the seam.

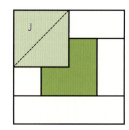 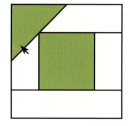

Repeat on the remaining corners.

Center Unit should measure 6 ½" x 6 ½".

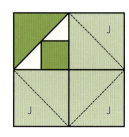 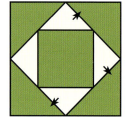

Make one.

Assemble Unit.

Partial Pineapple Round One Unit should measure 9 ½" x 9 ½".

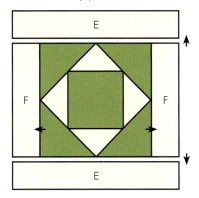 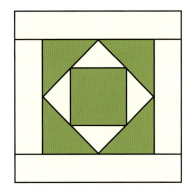

Make one.

Draw a diagonal line on the wrong side of the Fabric I squares.

With right sides facing, layer a Fabric I square on one corner of the Partial Pineapple Round One Unit.

Stitch on the drawn line and trim ¼" away from the seam.

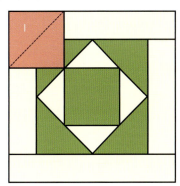 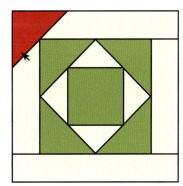

Repeat on the remaining corners.

Pineapple Round One Unit should measure 9 ½" x 9 ½".

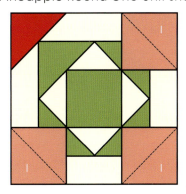 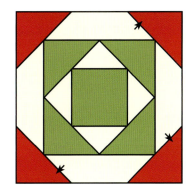

Make one.

Month One – Pineapple Block

Assemble Unit.

Partial Pineapple Round Two Unit should measure 12 ½" x 12 ½".

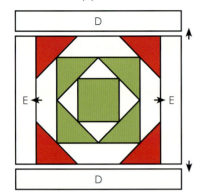 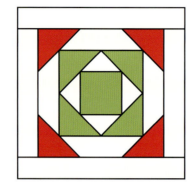

Make one.

With right sides facing, layer a Fabric I square on one corner of the Partial Pineapple Round Two Unit.

Stitch on the drawn line and trim ¼" away from the seam.

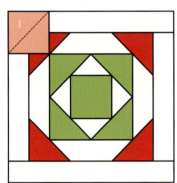 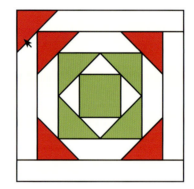

Repeat on the remaining corners.

Pineapple Round Two Unit should measure 12 ½" x 12 ½".

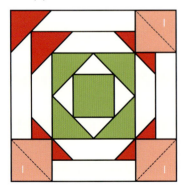 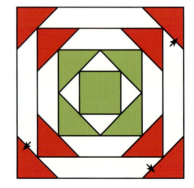

Make one.

Assemble Unit.

Partial Pineapple Round Three Unit should measure 15 ½" x 15 ½".

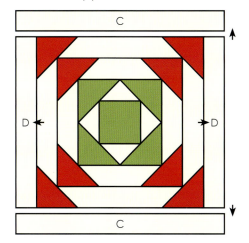 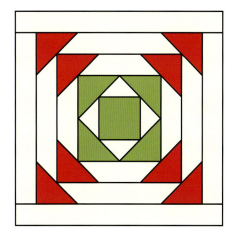

Make one.

Month One - Pineapple Block

With right sides facing, layer a Fabric I square on one corner of the Partial Pineapple Round Three Unit.

Stitch on the drawn line and trim ¼" away from the seam.

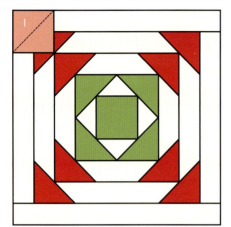
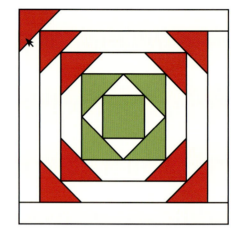

Repeat on the remaining corners.

Pineapple Round Three Unit should measure 15 ½" x 15 ½".

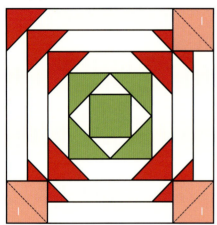
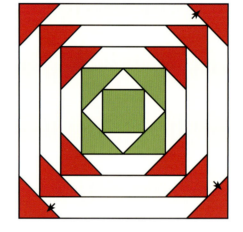

Make one.

Assemble Block.

Pineapple Block should measure 16 ½" x 16 ½".

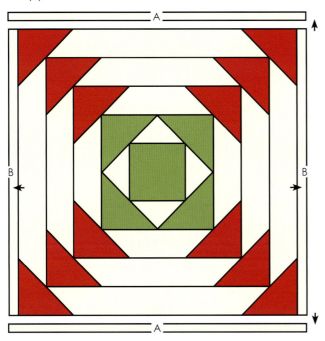

Make one.

Month Two – Flying Geese Criss Cross Block

Unfinished size: 16 ½" x 16 ½"
Make one

Cutting Instructions

Olive/Ivory Star Dot	
1 - 4 ½" x 42" strip, subcut into:	
1 - 4 ½" square	A
12 - 2 ½" x 4 ½" rectangles	B
1 - 2 ½" x 42" strip, subcut into:	
12 - 2 ½" squares	C
Red Star Dot	
3 - 2 ½" x 21" strips, subcut into:	
24 - 2 ½" squares	D
Green Scallop	
1 - 4 ½" x 21" strip, subcut into:	
4 - 2 ½" x 4 ½" rectangles	E
2 - 2 ½" x 21" strips, subcut into:	
4 - 2 ½" x 4 ½" rectangles	E
8 - 2 ½" squares	F

Block Instructions

Scallop print can be sewn all one direction or scrappy.

Draw a diagonal line on the wrong side of the Fabric D squares.

With right sides facing, layer a Fabric D square on one end of a Fabric B rectangle.

Stitch on the drawn line and trim ¼" away from the seam.

Repeat on the opposite end.

Flying Geese Unit should measure 2 ½" x 4 ½".

Make twelve.

Assemble Unit.

Middle Unit should measure 4 ½" x 6 ½".

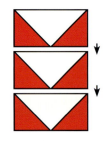 

Make four.

Assemble Unit.

Four Patch Unit should measure 4 ½" x 4 ½".

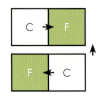

Make four.

Assemble Unit.

Corner Unit should measure 6 ½" x 6 ½".

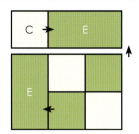

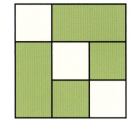

Make four.

Assemble Block.

Flying Geese Criss Cross Block should measure 16 ½" x 16 ½".

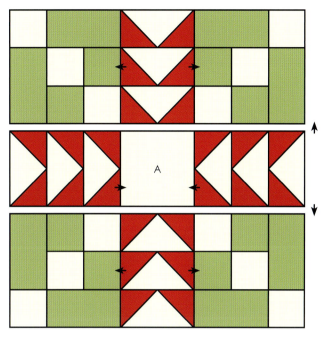

Make one.

Month Two – Feather Star Block

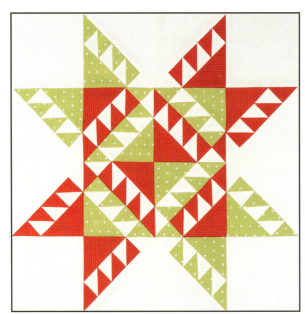

Unfinished size: 16 ½" x 16 ½"
Make one

Block Instructions

Press entire block open.

● ●

Cut on the diagonal once.

 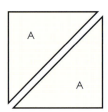

Make eight.

Make forty-eight.

Make eight.

Make twenty-four.

Make eight.

Make twenty-four.

Cutting Instructions

Ivory Tonal
1 - 5" x 42" strip, subcut into:
　4 - 5" squares   A
　From remainder of strip cut:
　4 - 4 ½" squares   B

1 - 3" x 42" strip, subcut into:
　3 - 3" squares   C

2 - 2 ¼" x 42" strips, subcut into:
　24 - 2 ¼" squares   D

Red Gingham
1 - 3 ½" x 21" strip, subcut into:
　4 - 3 ½" squares   E

1 - 3" x 21" strip, subcut into:
　3 - 3" squares   F

2 - 2 ¼" x 21" strips, subcut into:
　12 - 2 ¼" squares   G

Olive Star Dot
1 - 3 ½" x 21" strip, subcut into:
　4 - 3 ½" squares   H

1 - 3" x 21" strip, subcut into:
　3 - 3" squares   I

2 - 2 ¼" x 21" strips, subcut into:
　12 - 2 ¼" squares   J

Cut on the diagonal twice.

Make twelve.

Make twelve. You will not use two triangles.

Make twelve. You will not use two triangles.

Assemble Unit.

Trim Red Half Square Triangle Unit to measure 1 ⅝" x 1 ⅝".

Make twenty-four.

Assemble Unit.

Trim Green Half Square Triangle Unit to measure 1 ⅝" x 1 ⅝".

Make twenty-four.

Assemble Unit.

Trim Green Triangle Unit One to measure 4 ½" x 4 ½".

Make two.

Assemble Unit.

Trim Green Triangle Unit Two to measure 4 ½" x 4 ½".

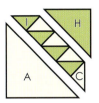

Make two.

Assemble Unit.

Trim Red Triangle Unit One to measure 4 ½" x 4 ½".

Make two.

Assemble Unit.

Trim Red Triangle Unit Two to measure 4 ½" x 4 ½".

Make two.

Month Two - Feather Star Block

Assemble Unit.

Trim Middle Triangle Unit One to measure 4 ½" x 4 ½".

Make two.

Assemble Unit.

Trim Middle Triangle Unit Two to measure 4 ½" x 4 ½".

Make two.

Assemble Block.

Feather Star Block should measure 16 ½" x 16 ½".

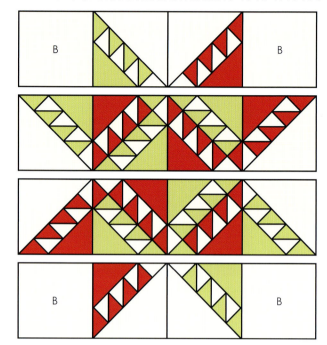

Make one.

Month Three - Nine Patchwork Block

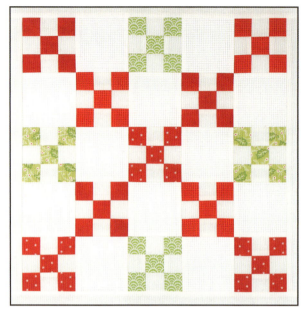

Unfinished size: 16 ½" x 16 ½"
Make one

Cutting Instructions

Ivory Tonal

4 - 1 ½" x 42" strips, subcut into:
5 - 1 ½" x 12" rectangles	A
10 - 1 ½" x 6" rectangles	B

2 - 1" x 42" strips, subcut into:
2 - 1" x 16 ½" rectangles	C
2 - 1" x 15 ½" rectangles	D

Ivory Gingham

2 - 3 ½" x 42" strips, subcut into:
12 - 3 ½" squares	E

From each Red Gingham, Red Tonal and Red Star Dot

2 - 1 ½" x 21" strips, subcut into:
2 - 1 ½" x 12" rectangles	F
1 - 1 ½" x 6" rectangle	G

From each Green Scallop and Olive Garland

2 - 1 ½" x 21" strips, subcut into:
2 - 1 ½" x 12" rectangles	H
1 - 1 ½" x 6" rectangle	I

Block Instructions

Assemble two matching Fabric F rectangles and one Fabric A rectangle.

Red Outside Strip Set should measure 3 ½" x 12".

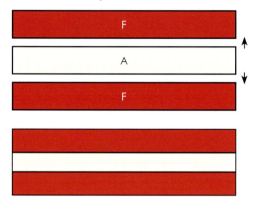

Make one from each red print.

Make three total.

Subcut each Red Outside Strip Set into six 1 ½" x 3 ½" rectangles.

Red Outside Nine Patch Unit should measure 1 ½" x 3 ½".

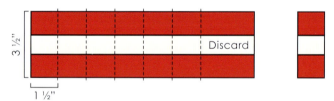

Make six from each red print.

Make eighteen total.

Assemble two Fabric B rectangles and one Fabric G rectangle.

Red Inside Strip Set should measure 3 ½" x 6".

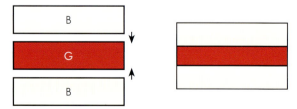

Make one from each red print.

Make three total.

Subcut each Red Inside Strip Set into three 1 ½" x 3 ½" rectangles.

Red Inside Nine Patch Unit should measure 1 ½" x 3 ½".

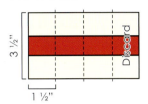

Make three from each red print.

Make nine total.

Assemble Unit using matching fabric.

Red Nine Patch Unit should measure 3 ½" x 3 ½".

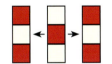

Make three from each red print.

Make nine total.

Assemble two matching Fabric H rectangles and one Fabric A rectangle.

Green Outside Strip Set should measure 3 ½" x 12".

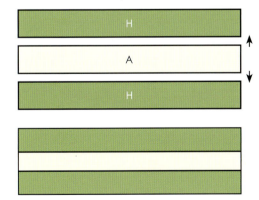

Make one from each green print.

Make two total.

Subcut each Green Outside Strip Set into four 1 ½" x 3 ½" rectangles.

Green Outside Nine Patch Unit should measure 1 ½" x 3 ½".

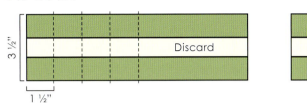

Make four from each green print.

Make eight total.

Assemble two Fabric B rectangles and one Fabric I rectangle.

Green Inside Strip Set should measure 3 ½" x 6".

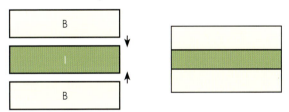

Make one from each green print.

Make two total.

Subcut each Green Inside Strip Set into two 1 ½" x 3 ½" rectangles.

Green Inside Nine Patch Unit should measure 1 ½" x 3 ½".

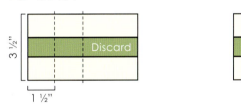

Make two from each green print.

Make four total.

Month Three – Nine Patchwork Block

Assemble Unit using matching fabric.

Green Nine Patch Unit should measure 3 ½" x 3 ½".

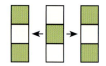

Make two from each green print.

Make four total.

Assemble Unit.

Nine Patchwork Unit should measure 15 ½" x 15 ½".

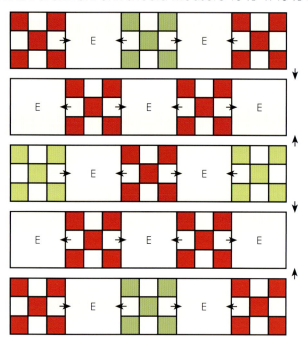

Make one.

Assemble Block.

Nine Patchwork Block should measure 16 ½" x 16 ½".

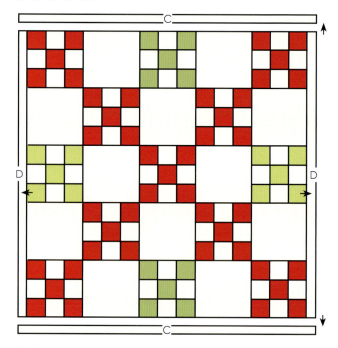

Make one.

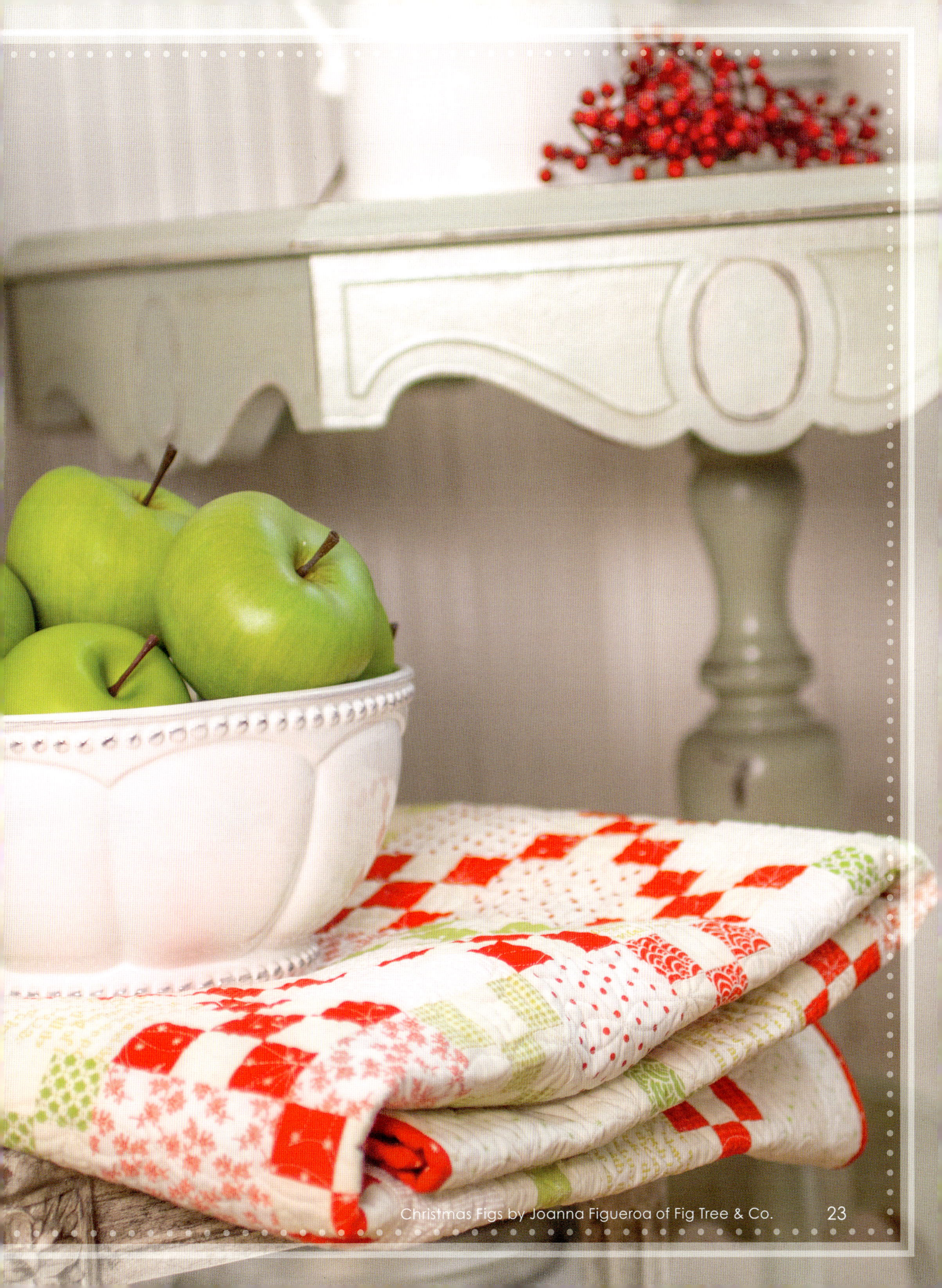

Month Three – Milky Way Block

Unfinished size: 16 ½" x 16 ½"
Make one

Cutting Instructions

Ivory Gingham		
1 - 3 ¼" x 42" strip, subcut into:		
4 - 3 ¼" squares		A
2 - 2 ¾" x 42" strips, subcut into:		
24 - 2 ¾" squares		B
Red/Ivory Star Dot		
4 - 1 ¾" x 21" strips, subcut into:		
2 - 1 ¾" x 16 ½" rectangles		C
2 - 1 ¾" x 14" rectangles		D
Red Star Dot		
1 - 2 ¾" x 21" strip, subcut into:		
4 - 2 ¾" squares		E
Green Tiles		
1 - 3 ¼" x 21" strip, subcut into:		
4 - 3 ¼" squares		F
3 - 2 ¾" x 21" strips, subcut into:		
12 - 2 ¾" x 5" rectangles		G

Block Instructions

Draw a diagonal line on the wrong side of the Fabric B squares.

With right sides facing, layer a Fabric B square on one end of a Fabric G rectangle.

Stitch on the drawn line and trim ¼" away from the seam.

Repeat on the opposite end.

Diagonal Unit should measure 2 ¾" x 5".

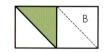

Make twelve.

Cut on the diagonal once.

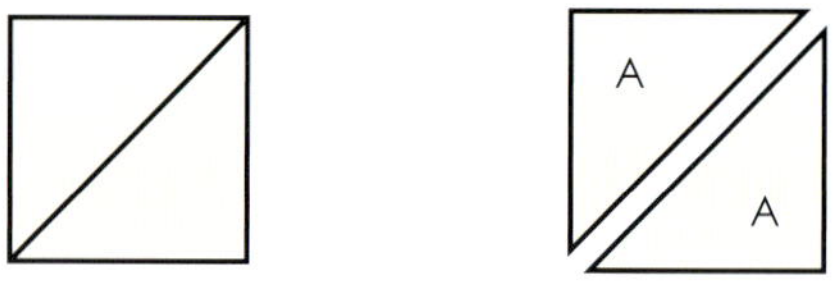

Make eight.

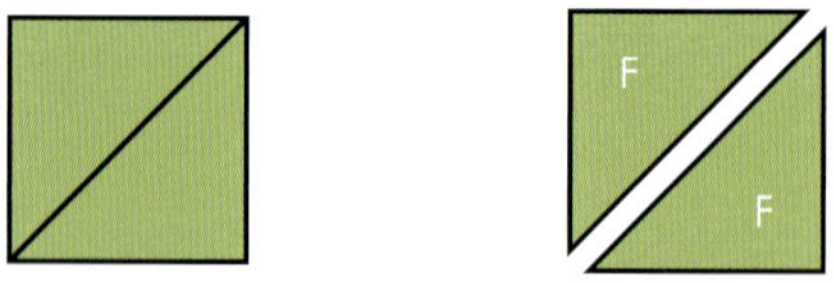

Make eight.

Assemble Unit.

Trim Half Square Triangle Unit to measure 2 ¾" x 2 ¾".

Make eight.

Assemble Unit.

Top Right Milky Way Unit should measure 5" x 5".

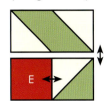

Make four.

Assemble Unit.

Partial Milky Way Unit should measure 7 ¼" x 7 ¼".

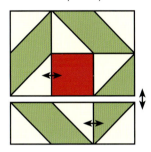 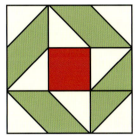

Make four.

Assemble Unit.

Milky Way Unit should measure 14" x 14".

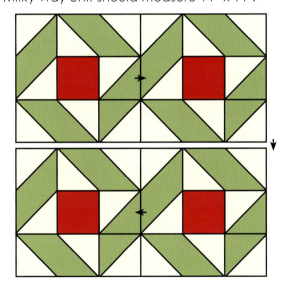

Make one.

Assemble Block.

Milky Way Block should measure 16 ½" x 16 ½".

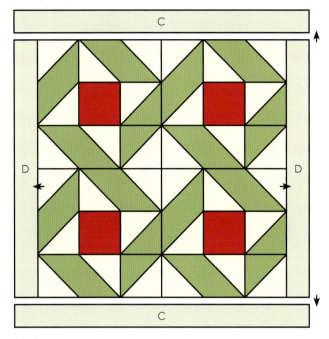

Make one.

Month Four – Lily Trio Block

Unfinished size: 16 ½" x 16 ½"
Make one

Cutting Instructions

Ivory Gingham
1 - 10 ½" x 42" strip, subcut into:
  1 - 10 ½" square — A
From remainder of strip cut:
  3 - 4" squares — B
  2 - 2 ½" x 7 ½" rectangles — C
  6 - 2 ¼" x 4" rectangles — D

Red Star Dot
1 - 4 ½" x 21" strip, subcut into:
  1 - 4 ½" square — E
From remainder of strip cut:
  4 - 2 ¼" x 4" rectangles — F

1 - 2 ¼" x 21" strip, subcut into:
  8 - 2 ¼" squares — G

Red Garland
1 - 4 ½" x 21" strip, subcut into:
  1 - 4 ½" square — E
From remainder of strip cut:
  2 - 2 ¼" x 4" rectangles — F
  4 - 2 ¼" squares — G

Green Gingham
1 - 12" x 21" strip, subcut into:
  1 - 12" square — H
From remainder of strip cut:
  2 - 4 ½" squares — I

½" Bias Tape Maker

Applique Glue

Block Instructions

Draw a diagonal line on the wrong side of the Fabric G squares.

With right sides facing, layer a Fabric G square on one end of a Fabric D rectangle.

Stitch on the drawn line and trim ¼" away from the seam.

Repeat on the opposite end with a matching Fabric G square.

Flying Geese Unit should measure 2 ¼" x 4".

Make four from the Red Star Dot fabric.

Make two from the Red Garland fabric.

Make six total.

Assemble Unit using matching fabric.

Partial Lily Trio Unit should measure 4" x 4".

Make four from the Red Star Dot fabric.

Make two from the Red Garland fabric.

Make six total.

Cut on the diagonal once.

Make two from the Red Star Dot fabric.

Make two from the Red Garland fabric. You will not use one triangle.

Make four. You will not use one triangle.

Assemble Unit.

Trim Half Square Triangle Unit to measure 4" x 4".

Make two from the Red Star Dot fabric.

Make one from the Red Garland fabric.

Make three total.

Assemble Unit using matching fabric.

Lily Trio Unit should measure 7 ½" x 7 ½".

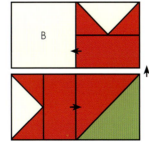 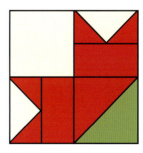

Make two from the Red Star Dot fabric.

Make one from the Red Garland fabric.

Make three total.

Month Four - Lily Trio Block

Assemble Unit.

Top Lily Trio Unit should measure 7 ½" x 16 ½".

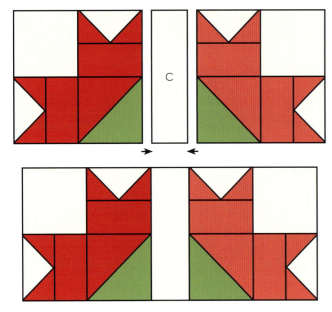

Make one.

● ● ● ● ● ● ● ● ● ● ● ● ● ● ● ● ● ●

Cut the Fabric H square into:

1 - 15" bias strip (H1)
2 - 7" bias strips (H2)

Using a ½" bias tape maker or your preferred method, create ½" bias tape from the Fabric H strips.

H1

Make one.

H2

Make two.

Draw a diagonal line on the right side of the Fabric A square.

On the Fabric A square, mark a dot 6 ½" down from the top right corner on the diagonal line as shown.

On the Fabric A square, mark dots 2 ¼" from the top right corner and ¼" in from the edge as shown.

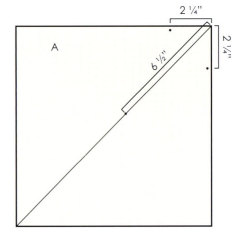

Make one.

● ● ● ● ● ● ● ● ● ● ● ● ● ● ● ● ● ●

Position the Fabric H2 strips on the Fabric A square from the drawn line to the marked dots. Make sure the inside edges of the Fabric H2 strips hit the dots.

Glue in place using applique glue.

Applique in place.

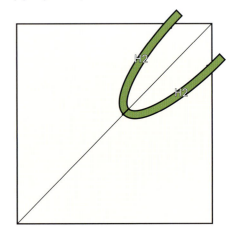

Make one.

Position the Fabric H1 strip on the drawn line.

Glue in place using applique glue.

Applique in place.

Make one.

Trim the Fabric H1 strip and Fabric H2 strips to the edge of the Fabric A square.

Trim Stem Unit on the left and bottom sides to measure 9 ½" x 9 ½".

Make one.

Assemble Unit.

Bottom Lily Trio Unit should measure 9 ½" x 16 ½".

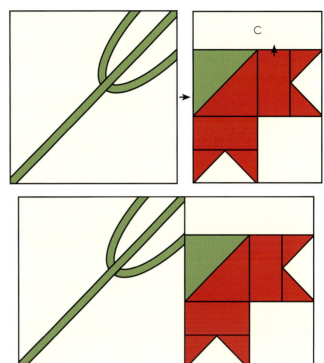

Make one.

Assemble Block.

Lily Trio Block should measure 16 ½" x 16 ½".

Make one.

Month Four - Pinwheel Swirl Block

Unfinished size: 16 ½" x 16 ½"
Make one

Cutting Instructions

Ivory Tonal		
3 - 3" x 21" strips, subcut into:		
	16 - 3" squares	A
Red/Ivory Star Dot		
2 - 2 ½" x 21" strips, subcut into:		
	16 - 2 ½" squares	B
Olive/Ivory Star Dot		
2 - 2 ½" x 21" strips, subcut into:		
	16 - 2 ½" squares	C
Red Tiles		
4 - 2 ½" x 21" strips, subcut into:		
	16 - 2 ½" x 4 ½" rectangles	D
Red Tonal		
2 - 3" x 21" strips, subcut into:		
	8 - 3" squares	E
Green Gingham		
2 - 3" x 21" strips, subcut into:		
	8 - 3" squares	F

Block Instructions

Draw a diagonal line on the wrong side of the Fabric B squares and Fabric C squares.

With right sides facing, layer a Fabric B square on the left end of a Fabric D rectangle.

Stitch on the drawn line and trim ¼" away from the seam.

Repeat on the right end with a Fabric C square.

Flying Geese Unit should measure 2 ½" x 4 ½".

Make sixteen.

Cut on the diagonal once.

Make thirty-two.

Make sixteen.

Make sixteen.

Assemble Unit.

Trim Red Half Square Triangle Unit to measure 2 ½" x 2 ½".

Make sixteen.

Assemble Unit.

Trim Green Half Square Triangle Unit to measure 2 ½" x 2 ½".

Make sixteen.

Assemble Unit.

Partial Pinwheel Swirl Unit should measure 4 ½" x 4 ½".

Make sixteen.

Assemble Unit.

Pinwheel Swirl Unit should measure 8 ½" x 8 ½".

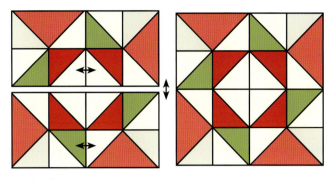

Make four.

Assemble Block.

Pinwheel Swirl Block should measure 16 ½" x 16 ½".

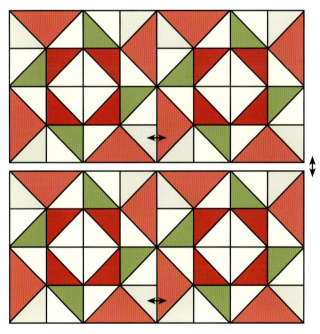

Make one.

Month Five - Bowties Block

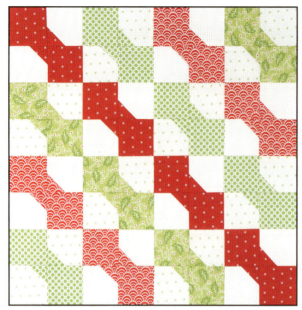

Unfinished size: 16 ½" x 16 ½"
Make one

Cutting Instructions

Ivory Gingham	
2 - 2 ½" x 21" strips, subcut into:	
16 - 2 ½" squares	A
Olive/Ivory Star Dot	
2 - 2 ½" x 21" strips, subcut into:	
16 - 2 ½" squares	B
From each Red Star Dot and Red Scallop	
1 - 2 ½" x 21" strip, subcut into:	
8 - 2 ½" squares	C
1 - 1 ½" x 21" strip, subcut into:	
8 - 1 ½" squares	D
From each Green Tiles and Olive Garland	
1 - 2 ½" x 21" strip, subcut into:	
8 - 2 ½" squares	E
1 - 1 ½" x 21" strip, subcut into:	
8 - 1 ½" squares	F

Block Instructions

Scallop print can be sewn all one direction or scrappy.

Draw a diagonal line on the wrong side of the Fabric D squares.

With right sides facing, layer a Fabric D square on the bottom left corner of a Fabric A square.

Stitch on the drawn line and trim ¼" away from the seam.

Partial Red Bowtie Unit should measure 2 ½" x 2 ½".

Make eight from each red print.

Make sixteen total.

Assemble Unit using matching fabric.

Red Bowtie Unit should measure 4 ½" x 4 ½".

Make four from each red print.

Make eight total.

Draw a diagonal line on the wrong side of the Fabric F squares.

With right sides facing, layer a Fabric F square on the bottom left corner of a Fabric B square.

Stitch on the drawn line and trim ¼" away from the seam.

Partial Green Bowtie Unit should measure 2 ½" x 2 ½".

Make eight from each green print.

Make sixteen total.

Assemble Unit using matching fabric.

Green Bowtie Unit should measure 4 ½" x 4 ½".

Make four from each green print.

Make eight total.

Assemble Block.

Bowties Block should measure 16 ½" x 16 ½".

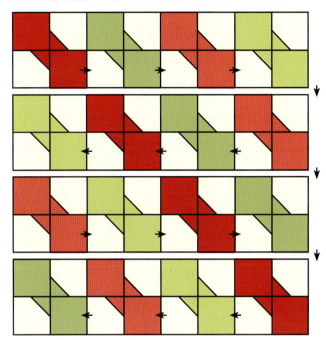

Make one.

Month Five – Tree of Life Block

Unfinished size: 16 ½" x 16 ½"
Make one

Cutting Instructions

Ivory Tonal
4 - 1 ½" x 21" strips, subcut into:
2 - 1 ½" x 16 ½" rectangles A
2 - 1 ½" x 14 ½" rectangles B

Ivory Star Dot
2 - 3" x 21" strips, subcut into:
8 - 3" squares C

Red/Ivory Star Dot
1 - 3" x 21" strip, subcut into:
6 - 3" squares D

Ivory Gingham
1 - 5 ½" x 21" strip, subcut into:
2 - 3 ½" x 5 ½" rectangles E
From remainder of strip cut:
1 - 5" square F

1 - 2 ½" x 21" strip, subcut into:
5 - 2 ½" squares G

Red Scallop
2 - 3" x 21" strips, subcut into:
10 - 3" squares H

Green Star Dot
1 - 5 ½" x 21" strip, subcut into:
1 - 5 ½" square I
From remainder of strip cut:
1 - 3 ½" square J

1 - 3" x 21" strip, subcut into:
4 - 3" squares K
From remainder of strip cut:
2 - 2" squares L
2 - 1 ½" squares M

Block Instructions

Scallop print can be sewn all one direction or scrappy.

• • • • • • • • • • • • • • • • • • •

Cut on the diagonal once.

Make sixteen.

Make twelve.

Make twenty.

Make eight.

• • • • • • • • • • • • • • • • • • •

Assemble Unit.

Trim Red Half Square Triangle Unit One to measure 2 ½" x 2 ½".

Make twelve.

Assemble Unit.

Trim Red Half Square Triangle Unit Two to measure 2 ½" x 2 ½".

Make eight.

• • • • • • • • • • • • • • • • • • •

Assemble Unit.

Trim Green Half Square Triangle Unit One to measure 2 ½" x 2 ½".

Make four.

• • • • • • • • • • • • • • • • • • •

Assemble Unit.

Trim Green Half Square Triangle Unit Two to measure 2 ½" x 2 ½".

Make four.

• • • • • • • • • • • • • • • • • • •

Assemble Unit.

Top Left Tree of Life Unit should measure 6 ½" x 6 ½".

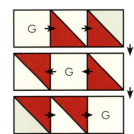 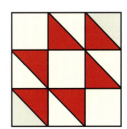

Make one.

Month Five - Tree of Life Block

Assemble Unit.

Top Right Tree of Life Unit should measure 6 ½" x 8 ½".

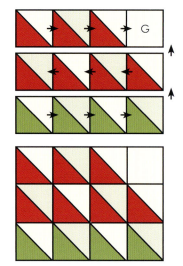

Make one.

Assemble Unit.

Bottom Left Tree of Life Unit should measure 6 ½" x 8 ½".

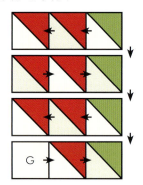 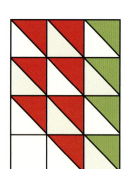

Make one.

Draw a diagonal line on the wrong side of the Fabric M squares and Fabric L squares.

With right sides facing, layer a Fabric M square on the top left corner of a Fabric E rectangle.

Stitch on the drawn line and trim ¼" away from the seam.

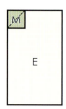 

Repeat on the top right corner with a Fabric L square.

Left Trunk Unit should measure 3 ½" x 5 ½".

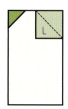 

Make one.

With right sides facing, layer a Fabric M square on the top left corner of a Fabric E rectangle.

Stitch on the drawn line and trim ¼" away from the seam.

Repeat on the bottom left corner with a Fabric L square.

Right Trunk Unit should measure 3 ½" x 5 ½".

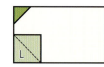 

Make one.

Draw a diagonal line on the wrong side of the Fabric F square.

With right sides facing, layer the Fabric F square on the bottom right corner of the Fabric I square.

Stitch on the drawn line and trim ¼" away from the seam.

Bottom Trunk Unit should measure 5 ½" x 5 ½".

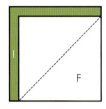 

Make one.

Assemble Unit.

Bottom Right Tree of Life Unit should measure 8 ½" x 8 ½".

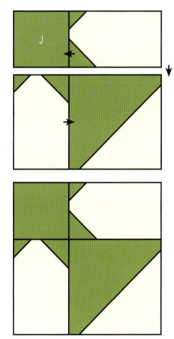

Make one.

Assemble Unit.

Tree of Life Unit should measure 14 ½" x 14 ½".

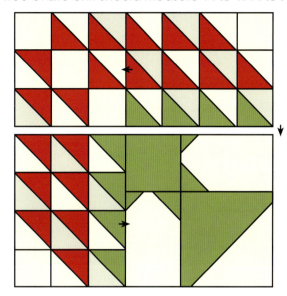

Make one.

Assemble Block.

Tree of Life Block should measure 16 ½" x 16 ½".

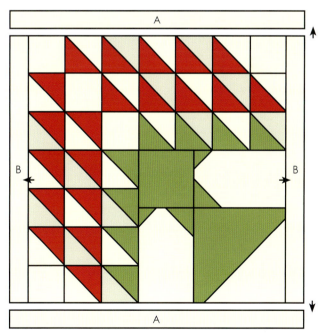

Make one.

Month Six – Birds in the Air Block

Unfinished size: 16 ½" x 16 ½"
Make one

Block Instructions

Scallop print can be sewn all one direction or scrappy.

Cut on the diagonal once.

Make forty.

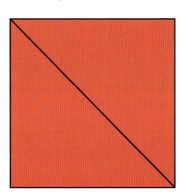

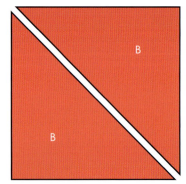

Make four.

Make four from each green print.

Make twenty-four total.

Cutting Instructions

Olive/Ivory Star Dot		
4 - 3" x 21" strips, subcut into:		
20 - 3" squares		A
Berry Scallop		
1 - 9" x 21" strip, subcut into:		
2 - 9" squares		B
From each Green Scallop, Green Gingham, Olive Gingham, Olive Star Dot, Green Tiles and Green Star Dot		
2 - 3" squares		C

Assemble Unit.

Trim Half Square Triangle Unit to measure 2 ½" x 2 ½".

Make four from each green print.

Make twenty-four total.

Assemble Unit.

Trim ¼" away from the left side.

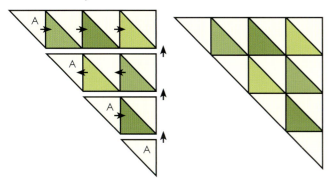

Make four Partial Birds in the Air Units.

Assemble Unit.

Trim Birds in the Air Unit to measure 8 ½" x 8 ½".

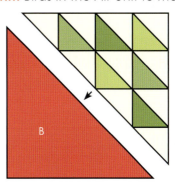

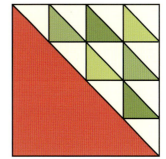

Make four.

Assemble Block.

Birds in the Air Block should measure 16 ½" x 16 ½".

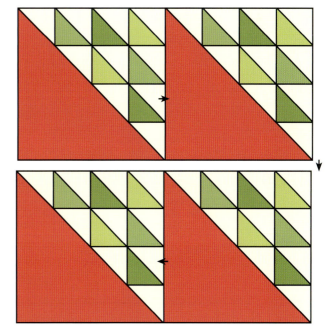

Make one.

Month Six – Goose in the Pond Block

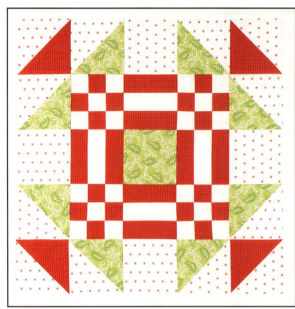

Unfinished size: 16 ½" x 16 ½"
Make one

Cutting Instructions

Ivory Tonal		
3 - 1 ½" x 21" strips		A
4 - 1" x 21" strips, subcut into:		
2 - 1" x 16 ½" rectangles		B
2 - 1" x 15 ½" rectangles		C
Red/Ivory Star Dot		
2 - 4" x 21" strips, subcut into:		
6 - 4" squares		D
From remainder of strip cut:		
4 - 3 ½" squares		E
Red Gingham		
1 - 4" x 21" strip, subcut into:		
2 - 4" squares		F
3 - 1 ½" x 21"strips		G
Olive Garland		
1 - 4" x 21" strip, subcut into:		
4 - 4" squares		H
From remainder of strip cut:		
1 - 3 ½" square		I

Block Instructions

Cut on the diagonal once.

Make twelve.

Make four.

Make eight.

Assemble Unit.

Trim Red Half Square Triangle Unit to measure 3 ½" x 3 ½".

Make four.

Assemble Unit.

Trim Green Half Square Triangle Unit to measure 3 ½" x 3 ½".

Make eight.

Assemble Unit.

Outside Goose in the Pond Unit should measure 3 ½" x 9 ½".

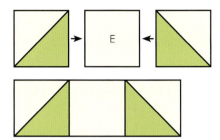

Make four.

Assemble two Fabric A strips and one Fabric G strip.

Ivory Strip Set should measure 3 ½" x 21".

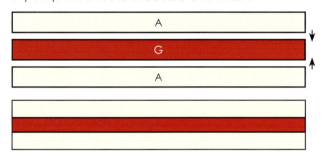

Make one.

Subcut the Ivory Strip Set into eight 1 ½" x 3 ½" rectangles.

Ivory Nine Patch Unit should measure 1 ½" x 3 ½".

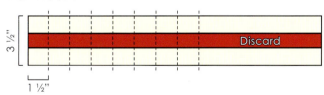

Make eight.

Assemble two Fabric G strips and one Fabric A strip.

Red Strip Set should measure 3 ½" x 21".

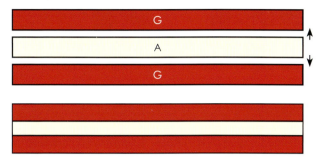

Make one.

Subcut the Red Strip Set into four 3 ½" squares and four 1 ½" x 3 ½" rectangles.

Rail Fence Unit should measure 3 ½" x 3 ½".

Red Nine Patch Unit should measure 1 ½" x 3 ½".

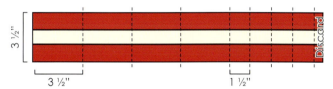

Make four.

Make four.

Month Six – Goose in the Pond Block

Assemble Unit.

Nine Patch Unit should measure 3 ½" x 3 ½".

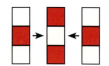

Make four.

Assemble Unit.

Center Goose in the Pond Unit should measure 9 ½" x 9 ½".

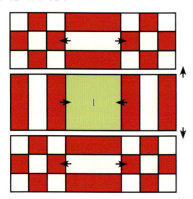

Make one.

Assemble Unit.

Goose in the Pond Unit should measure 15 ½" x 15 ½".

Make one.

Assemble Block.

Goose in the Pond Block should measure 16 ½" x 16 ½".

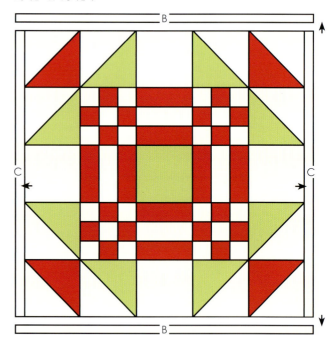

Make one.

Month Seven - Carolina Lily Block

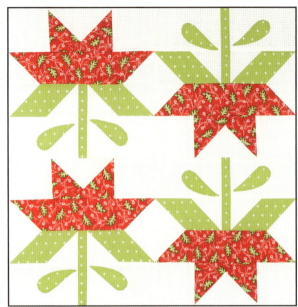

Unfinished size: 16 ½" x 16 ½"
Make one

Cutting Instructions

Ivory Gingham	
2 - 3 ¾" x 42" strips, subcut into:	
8 - 3 ¾" x 5 ¼" rectangles	A
1 - 2 ¾" x 42" strip, subcut into:	
4 - 2 ¾" x 4" rectangles	B
8 - 2 ¾" squares	C
2 - 2 ¼" x 42" strips, subcut into:	
24 - 2 ¼" squares	D

 Red Garland	
2 - 2 ¾" x 21" strips, subcut into:	
8 - 2 ¾" squares	E
2 - 2 ¼" x 21" strips, subcut into:	
4 - 2 ¼" x 8 ½" rectangles	F

 Olive Star Dot	
1 - 3" x 21" strip	G
8 - applique pieces	
2 - 2 ¼" x 21" strips, subcut into:	
8 - 2 ¼" x 4 ¼" rectangles	H
1 - 1" x 21" strip, subcut into:	
4 - 1" x 4 ½" rectangles	I

Block Instructions

Draw a diagonal line on the wrong side of the Fabric E squares.

With right sides facing, layer a Fabric E square on one end of a Fabric B rectangle.

Stitch on the drawn line and trim ¼" away from the seam.

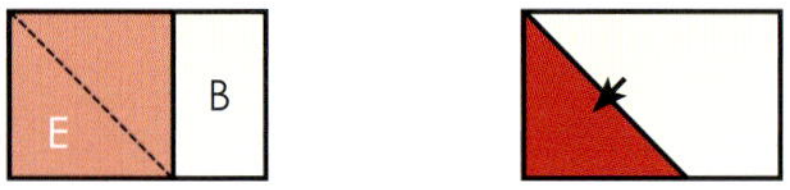

Repeat on the opposite end.

Top Carolina Lily Unit should measure 2 ¾" x 4".

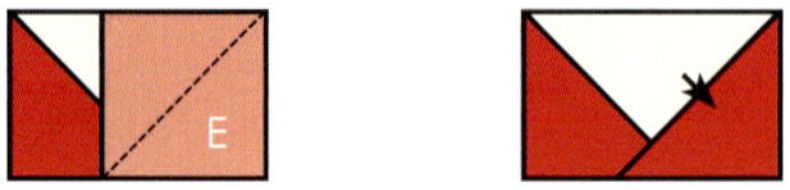

Make four.

Draw a diagonal line on the wrong side of the Fabric D squares.

With right sides facing, layer a Fabric D square on one end of a Fabric F rectangle.

Stitch on the drawn line and trim ¼" away from the seam.

Repeat on the opposite end.

Middle Carolina Lily Unit should measure 2 ¼" x 8 ½".

Make four.

With right sides facing, layer a Fabric D square on one end of a Fabric H rectangle.

Stitch on the drawn line and trim ¼" away from the seam.

Repeat on the opposite end.

Top Left Leaf Unit should measure 2 ¼" x 4 ¼".

Make four.

With right sides facing, layer a Fabric D square on one end of a Fabric H rectangle.

Stitch on the drawn line and trim ¼" away from the seam.

Repeat on the opposite end.

Top Right Leaf Unit should measure 2 ¼" x 4 ¼".

Make four.

Using the Left Carolina Lily Leaf Template on page 47, cut four Left Carolina Lily Leaf Units from the Fabric G strip.

Applique a Left Carolina Lily Leaf Unit on a Fabric A rectangle using the placement guide on page 47.

Using the trim line on page 47, **trim** Bottom Left Leaf Unit to measure 2 ¾" x 4 ¼".

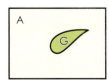

Make four.

Using the Right Carolina Lily Leaf Template on page 47, cut four Right Carolina Lily Leaf Units from the Fabric G strip.

Applique a Right Carolina Lily Leaf Unit on a Fabric A rectangle using the placement guide on page 47.

Using the trim line on page 47, **trim** Bottom Right Leaf Unit to measure 2 ¾" x 4 ¼".

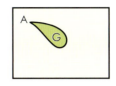

Make four.

Assemble Unit.

Leaf Unit should measure 4 ½" x 8 ½".

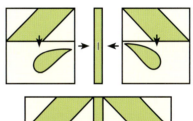

Make four.

Month Seven - Carolina Lily Block

Assemble Unit.

Carolina Lily Unit should measure 8 ½" x 8 ½".

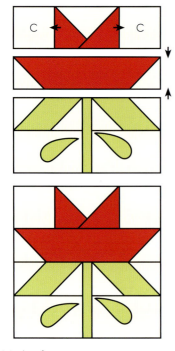

Make four.

Assemble Block.

Carolina Lily Block should measure 16 ½" x 16 ½".

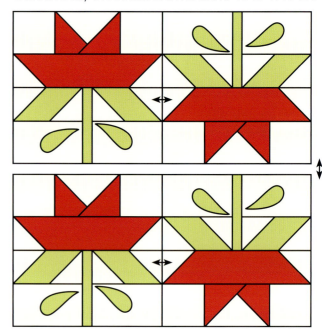

Make one.

Left Carolina Lily Leaf Template and Placement Guide

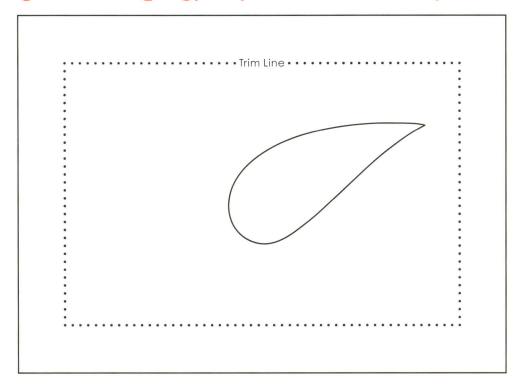

Trim Line

Right Carolina Lily Leaf Template and Placement Guide

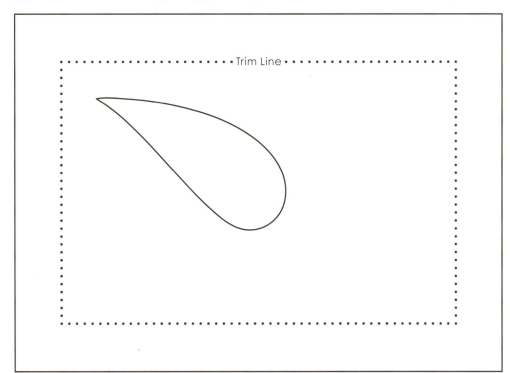

Trim Line

Month Seven - Bear Paw Block

Unfinished size: 16 ½" x 16 ½"
Make one

Cutting Instructions

Ivory Gingham	
1 - 3" x 42" strip, subcut into:	
4 - 3" x 7 ¼" rectangles	A
From remainder of strip cut:	
4 - 2 ¾" squares	B
From each Red/Ivory Star Dot and Ivory Star Dot	
4 - 3 ¼" squares	C
Red Gingham	
2 - 3 ¼" x 21" strips, subcut into:	
8 - 3 ¼" squares	D
From remainder of strip cut:	
1 - 3" square	E
Red Tiles	
1 - 5 ½" x 21" strip, subcut into:	
4 - applique pieces	F
Green Scallop	
1 - 5" x 21" strip, subcut into:	
4 - 5" squares	G

Block Instructions

Scallop print can be sewn all one direction or scrappy.

Cut on the diagonal once.

Make eight from each ivory print.

Make sixteen total.

Make sixteen.

Assemble Unit.

Trim Half Square Triangle Unit to measure 2 ¾" x 2 ¾".

Make eight from each ivory print.

Make sixteen total.

Assemble Unit.

Top Bear Paw Unit should measure 2 ¾" x 5".

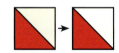

Make four.

Assemble Unit.

Left Bear Paw Unit should measure 2 ¾" x 5".

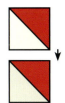

Make four.

Assemble Unit.

Partial Bear Paw Unit should measure 7 ¼" x 7 ¼".

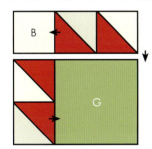 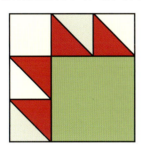

Make four.

Assemble Unit.

Bear Paw Unit should measure 16 ½" x 16 ½".

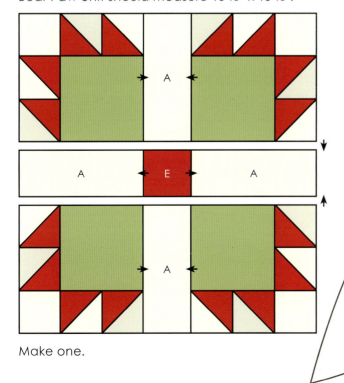

Make one.

Using the Bear Paw Flourish Template, cut four Bear Paw Flourish Units from the Fabric F strip.

Applique Bear Paw Flourish Units on the Bear Paw Unit, centering on the Fabric G squares.

Bear Paw Block should measure 16 ½" x 16 ½".

Make one.

Bear Paw Flourish Template

Month Eight – Flying Geese Block

Unfinished size: 16 ½" x 16 ½"
Make one

Cutting Instructions

From each Ivory Tonal, Red/Ivory Star Dot, Ivory Gingham and Ivory Star Dot

2 - 2 ½" x 21" strips, subcut into:
  8 - 2 ½" x 4 ½" rectangles   A

From each Red Scallop, Berry Gingham, Red Star Dot and Red Tiles

1 - 2 ½" x 21" strip, subcut into:
  8 - 2 ½" squares   B

From each Green Tiles, Green Star Dot, Olive Gingham and Green Scallop

1 - 2 ½" x 21" strip, subcut into:
  8 - 2 ½" squares   C

Block Instructions

Scallop print can be sewn all one direction or scrappy.

· · · · · · · · · · · · · · · · · · · ·

Draw a diagonal line on the wrong side of the Fabric B squares.

With right sides facing, layer a Fabric B square on one end of a Fabric A rectangle.

Stitch on the drawn line and trim ¼" away from the seam.

Repeat on the opposite end with a matching Fabric B square.

Red Flying Geese Unit should measure 2 ½" x 4 ½".

Make four from each red print.

Make sixteen total.

· · · · · · · · · · · · · · · · · · · ·

Draw a diagonal line on the wrong side of the Fabric C squares.

With right sides facing, layer a Fabric C square on one end of a Fabric A rectangle.

Stitch on the drawn line and trim ¼" away from the seam.

Repeat on the opposite end with a matching Fabric C square.

Green Flying Geese Unit should measure 2 ½" x 4 ½".

Make four from each green print.

Make sixteen total.

Assemble Unit.

Flying Geese Unit should measure 8 ½" x 8 ½".

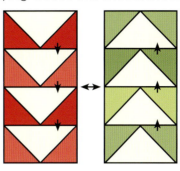

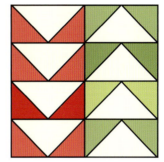

Make four.

· · · · · · · · · · · · · · · · · · · ·

Assemble Block.

Flying Geese Block should measure 16 ½" x 16 ½".

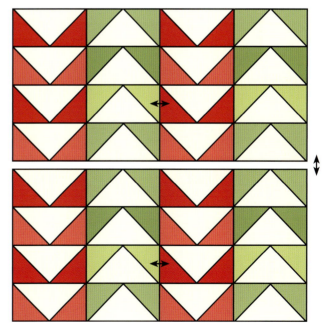

Make one.

Month Eight - Rolling Stones Block

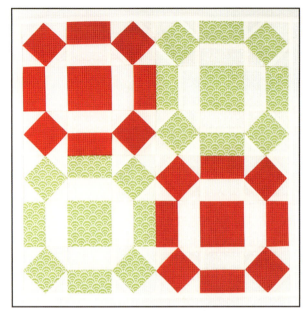

Unfinished size: 16 ½" x 16 ½"
Make one

Cutting Instructions

Ivory Tonal
5 - 1 ¾" x 21" strips, subcut into:
    48 - 1 ¾" squares   A
4 - 1" x 21" strips, subcut into:
    2 - 1" x 16 ½" rectangles   B
    2 - 1" x 15 ½" rectangles   C

Ivory Star Dot
4 - 1 ¾" x 21" strips, subcut into:
    16 - 1 ¾" x 3" rectangles   D
    16 - 1 ¾" squares   E

Red Gingham
3 - 3" x 21" strips, subcut into:
    10 - 3" squares   F
    8 - 1 ¾" x 3" rectangles   G

Green Scallop
2 - 3" x 21" strips, subcut into:
    10 - 3" squares   H
    4 - 1 ¾" x 3" rectangles   I
1 - 1 ¾" x 21" strip, subcut into:
    4 - 1 ¾" x 3" rectangles   I

Block Instructions

Scallop print can be sewn all one direction or scrappy.

Draw a diagonal line on the wrong side of the Fabric A squares and Fabric E squares.

With right sides facing, layer a Fabric E square on the bottom right corner of a Fabric F square.

Stitch on the drawn line and trim ¼" away from the seam.

Repeat on the remaining corners with Fabric A squares.

Red Snowball Unit should measure 3" x 3".

Make eight.

Assemble Unit.

Red Two Patch Unit should measure 3" x 3".

Make eight.

Assemble Unit.

Red Rolling Stone Unit should measure 8" x 8".

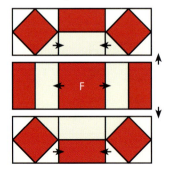

Make two.

With right sides facing, layer a Fabric E square on the bottom right corner of a Fabric H square.

Stitch on the drawn line and trim ¼" away from the seam.

Repeat on the remaining corners with Fabric A squares.

Green Snowball Unit should measure 3" x 3".

Make eight.

Assemble Unit.

Green Two Patch Unit should measure 3" x 3".

Make eight.

Assemble Unit.

Green Rolling Stone Unit should measure 8" x 8".

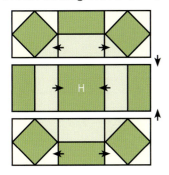

Make two.

Assemble Unit.

Rolling Stones Unit should measure 15 ½" x 15 ½".

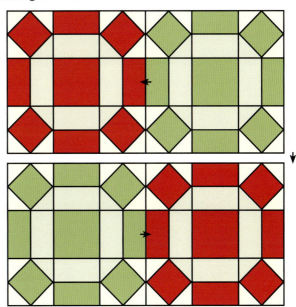

Make one.

Assemble Block.

Rolling Stones Block should measure 16 ½" x 16 ½".

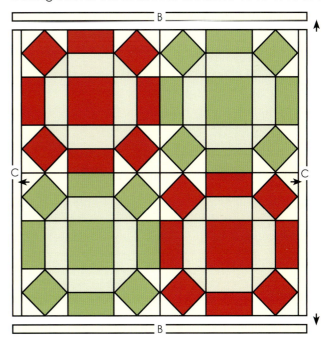

Make one.

Month Nine – Peppermint Block

Unfinished size: 16 ½" x 16 ½"
Make one

Cutting Instructions

Ivory Tonal		
3 - 1 ¾" x 42" strips, subcut into:		
64 - 1 ¾" squares		A
1 - 3" x 42" strip, subcut into:		
8 - 3" squares		B
Ivory Star Dot		
2 - 3" x 21" strips, subcut into:		
8 - 3" squares		B
From each Ivory Gingham and Olive/Ivory Star Dot		
2 - 3" x 21" strips, subcut into:		
8 - 3" squares		C
From each Berry Gingham and Red Tiles		
2 - 3" x 21" strips, subcut into:		
8 - 3" squares		D
From each Olive Star Dot and Green Scallop		
2 - 3" x 21" strips, subcut into:		
8 - 3" squares		E

Block Instructions

Scallop print can be sewn all one direction or scrappy.

• •

Pair a Fabric B square with a Fabric D square for the Red Peppermint Units (red pair).

Pair a Fabric C square with a Fabric E square for the Green Peppermint Units (green pair).

• •

Cut on the diagonal once.

Make sixteen from each ivory print.

Make thirty-two total.

Make sixteen from each ivory print.

Make thirty-two total.

Make sixteen from each red print.

Make thirty-two total.

Make sixteen from each green print.

Make thirty-two total.

Assemble Unit.

Trim Red Half Square Triangle Unit to measure 2 ½" x 2 ½".

Make sixteen from each red pair.

Make thirty-two total.

Assemble Unit using matching fabric.

Partial Red Peppermint Unit should measure 4 ½" x 4 ½".

Make four from each red pair.

Make eight total.

Draw a diagonal line on the wrong side of the Fabric A squares.

With right sides facing, layer a Fabric A square on one corner of a Partial Red Peppermint Unit.

Stitch on the drawn line and trim ¼" away from the seam.

Repeat on the remaining corners.

Red Peppermint Unit should measure 4 ½" x 4 ½".

Make four from each red pair.

Make eight total.

Assemble Unit.

Trim Green Half Square Triangle Unit to measure 2 ½" x 2 ½".

Make sixteen from each green pair.

Make thirty-two total.

Assemble Unit using matching fabric.

Partial Green Peppermint Unit should measure 4 ½" x 4 ½".

Make four from each green pair.

Make eight total.

With right sides facing, layer a Fabric A square on one corner of a Partial Green Peppermint Unit.

Stitch on the drawn line and trim ¼" away from the seam.

Repeat on the remaining corners.

Green Peppermint Unit should measure 4 ½" x 4 ½".

Make four from each green pair.

Make eight total.

Month Nine – Peppermint Block

Assemble Unit using four different Units.

Peppermint Unit should measure 8 ½" x 8 ½".

Assemble Block.

Peppermint Block should measure 16 ½" x 16 ½".

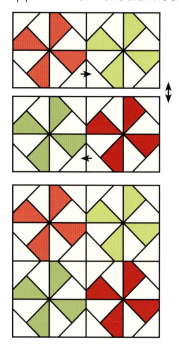

Make four.

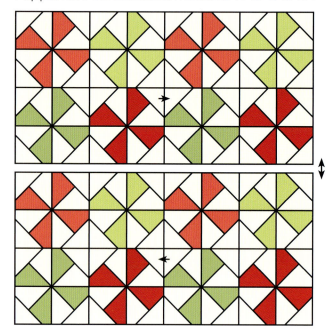

Make one.

Month Nine – Christmas Star Block

Unfinished size: 16 ½" x 16 ½"
Make one

Block Instructions

Draw a diagonal line on the wrong side of the Fabric F squares.

With right sides facing, layer a Fabric F square on one end of a Fabric B rectangle.

Stitch on the drawn line and trim ¼" away from the seam.

Repeat on the opposite end.

Flying Geese Unit should measure 2 ½" x 4 ½".

Make four.

Cutting Instructions

Ivory Tonal	
1 - 4 ½" x 42" strip, subcut into:	
8 - 4 ½" squares	A
2 - 2 ½" x 42" strips, subcut into:	
4 - 2 ½" x 4 ½" rectangles	B
12 - 2 ½" squares	C
Red/Ivory Star Dot	
1 - 2 ½" x 21" strip, subcut into:	
8 - 2 ½" squares	D
Red Gingham	
2 - 2 ½" x 42" strips, subcut into:	
8 - 2 ½" x 4 ½" rectangles	E
8 - 2 ½" squares	F
Green Star Dot	
2 - 2 ½" squares	G
Green Gingham	
2 - 2 ½" squares	H

Assemble Unit.

Four Patch Unit should measure 4 ½" x 4 ½".

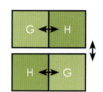

Make one.

Assemble Unit.

Center Unit should measure 8 ½" x 8 ½".

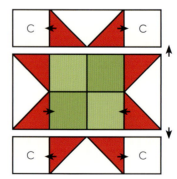

Make one.

Draw a diagonal line on the wrong side of the remaining Fabric C squares and Fabric D squares.

With right sides facing, layer a Fabric C square on the top end of a Fabric E rectangle.

Stitch on the drawn line and trim ¼" away from the seam.

Repeat on the bottom end with a Fabric D square.

Left Star Point Unit should measure 2 ½" x 4 ½".

Make four.

With right sides facing, layer a Fabric C square on the top end of a Fabric E rectangle.

Stitch on the drawn line and trim ¼" away from thc scam.

Repeat on the bottom end with a Fabric D square.

Right Star Point Unit should measure 2 ½" x 4 ½".

Make four.

Assemble Unit.

Outside Christmas Star Unit should measure 4 ½" x 8 ½".

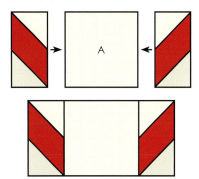

Make four.

Assemble Block.

Christmas Star Block should measure 16 ½" x 16 ½".

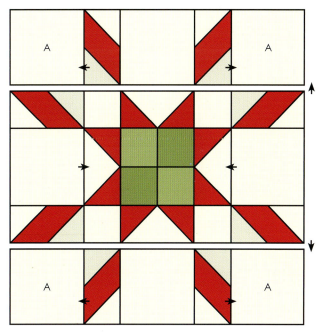

Make one.

Month Ten - Little Red Schoolhouse Block

Unfinished size: 16 ½" x 16 ½"
Make one

Cutting Instructions

Ivory Tonal

1 - 1" x 21" strip, subcut into:
  1 - 1" x 16 ½" rectangle   A

From each Ivory Gingham and Olive/Ivory Star Dot

2 - 2 ½" x 21" strips, subcut into:
  1 - 2 ½" square   B
  From remainder of strips cut:
  2 - 2" x 3 ¾" rectangles   C
  2 - 2" x 2 ¾" rectangles   D
  6 - 2" squares   E

2 - 1 ½" x 21" strips, subcut into:
  2 - 1 ½" x 8 ¼" rectangles   F
  2 - 1 ½" x 3 ¼" rectangles   G
  4 - 1 ½" x 2" rectangles   H

1 - 1 ¼" x 21" strip, subcut into:
  4 - 1 ¼" x 4 ½" rectangles   I

From each Red Star Dot and Red Tonal

1 - 2 ½" x 21" strip, subcut into:
  1 - 2 ½" square   J
  From remainder of strip cut:
  2 - 2" x 4 ½" rectangles   K

1 - 2" x 21" strip, subcut into:
  4 - 2" squares   L

1 - 1 ¾" x 21" strip, subcut into:
  2 - 1 ¾" x 3 ½" rectangles   M
  From remainder of strip cut:
  2 - 1 ½" x 4 ½" rectangles   N

1 - 1 ½" x 21" strip, subcut into:
  4 - 1 ½" x 3 ¼" rectangles   O

2 - 1 ¼" x 21" strips, subcut into:
  2 - 1 ¼" x 4 ½" rectangles   P
  6 - 1 ¼" x 2" rectangles   Q

1 - 1 ⅛" x 21" strip, subcut into:
  4 - 1 ⅛" x 2" rectangles   R

Block Instructions

Pair an Ivory Print with a Red Print for the Little Red Schoolhouse Units (pair).

Assemble Unit using matching fabric.

Chimney Unit should measure 2" x 8 ¼".

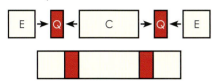

Make two from each pair.

Make four total.

Cut on the diagonal once.

Make two from each ivory print.

Make four total.

Make two from each red print.

Make four total.

Assemble Unit.

Trim Half Square Triangle Unit to measure 2" x 2".

Make two from each pair.

Make four total.

Draw a diagonal line on the wrong side of the Fabric L squares.

With right sides facing, layer a Fabric L square on one end of a Fabric D rectangle.

Stitch on the drawn line and trim ¼" away from the seam.

Repeat on the opposite end with a matching Fabric L square.

Middle Roof Unit should measure 2" x 2 ¾".

Make two from each pair.

Make four total.

Draw a diagonal line on the wrong side of the remaining Fabric E squares.

With right sides facing, layer a Fabric E square on the right end of a Fabric K rectangle.

Stitch on the drawn line and trim ¼" away from the seam.

Right Roof Unit should measure 2" x 4 ½".

Make two from each pair.

Make four total.

Assemble Unit using matching fabric.

Roof Unit should measure 2" x 8 ¼".

Make two from each pair.

Make four total.

Month Ten - Little Red Schoolhouse Block

Assemble Unit using matching fabric.

Door Unit should measure 3 ½" x 4 ½".

Make two from each pair.

Make four total.

Assemble Unit using matching fabric.

Partial Window Unit should measure 4 ½" x 4 ½".

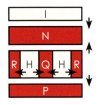

Make two from each pair.

Make four total.

Assemble Unit using matching fabric.

Window Unit should measure 4 ½" x 8 ¼".

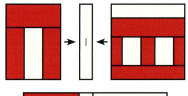

Make two from each pair.

Make four total.

Assemble Unit using matching fabric.

Little Red Schoolhouse Unit should measure 8 ¼" x 8 ½".

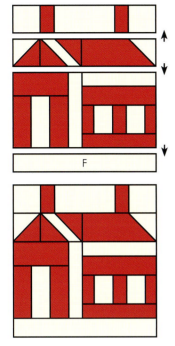

Make two from each pair.

Make four total.

Assemble Block.

Little Red Schoolhouse Block should measure 16 ½" x 16 ½".

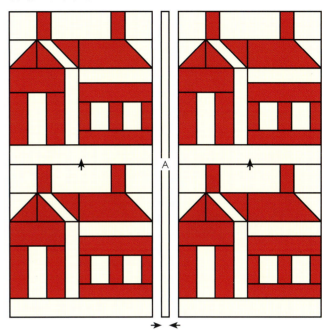

Make one.

Month Ten - Little Spools Block

Unfinished size: 16 ½" x 16 ½"
Make one

Cutting Instructions

Ivory Gingham		
2 - 1 ½" x 21" strips		A
3 - 1 ½" x 21" strips, subcut into:		
32 - 1 ½" squares		B
Red/Ivory Star Dot		
2 - 1 ½" x 21" strips		C
3 - 1 ½" x 21" strips, subcut into:		
32 - 1 ½" squares		D
Red Star Dot		
1 - 2 ½" x 21" strip		E
Red Scallop		
2 - 4 ½" x 21" strips, subcut into:		
16 - 1 ½" x 4 ½" rectangles		F
Green Tiles		
1 - 2 ½" x 21" strip		G
Olive Garland		
2 - 4 ½" x 21" strips, subcut into:		
16 - 1 ½" x 4 ½" rectangles		H

Block Instructions

Scallop print can be sewn all one direction or scrappy.

Draw a diagonal line on the wrong side of the Fabric B squares.

With right sides facing, layer a Fabric B square on one end of a Fabric H rectangle.

Stitch on the drawn line and trim ¼" away from the seam.

Repeat on the opposite end.

Olive Outer Spool Unit should measure 1 ½" x 4 ½".

Make sixteen.

Assemble two Fabric A strips and the Fabric E strip.

Red Strip Set should measure 4 ½" x 21".

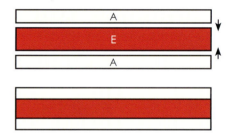

Make one.

Subcut the Red Strip Set into eight 2 ½" x 4 ½" rectangles.

Red Inner Spool Unit should measure 2 ½" x 4 ½".

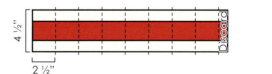

Make eight.

Assemble Unit.

Red Spool Unit should measure 4 ½" x 4 ½".

Make eight.

Draw a diagonal line on the wrong side of the Fabric D squares.

With right sides facing, layer a Fabric D square on the top end of a Fabric F rectangle.

Stitch on the drawn line and trim ¼" away from the seam.

Repeat on the bottom end.

Red Outer Spool Unit should measure 1 ½" x 4 ½".

Make sixteen.

Assemble two Fabric C strips and the Fabric G strip.

Green Strip Set should measure 4 ½" x 21".

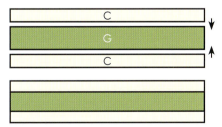

Make one.

Subcut the Green Strip Set into eight 2 ½" x 4 ½" rectangles.

Green Inner Spool Unit should measure 2 ½" x 4 ½".

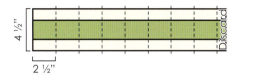

Make eight.

Assemble Unit.

Green Spool Unit should measure 4 ½" x 4 ½".

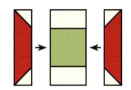

Make eight.

Assemble Block.

Little Spools Block should measure 16 ½" x 16 ½".

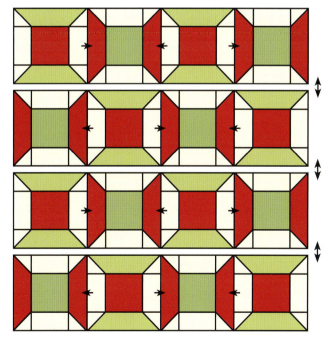

Make one.

Month Eleven - Cornerstone Blocks

Unfinished size: 2 ½" x 2 ½"
Make thirty

Cutting Instructions

Red Star Dot 5 - 1 ½" x 21" strips		A
Olive Gingham 5 - 1 ½" x 21" strips		B

Block Instructions

Assemble one Fabric A strip and one Fabric B strip.

Strip Set should measure 2 ½" x 21".

Make five.

Subcut each Strip Set into twelve 1 ½" x 2 ½" rectangles.

Partial Cornerstone Unit should measure 1 ½" x 2 ½".

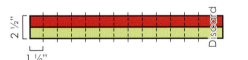

Make sixty.

Assemble Block.

Cornerstone Block should measure 2 ½" x 2 ½".

Make thirty.

Month Twelve - Finishing

Cutting Instructions

78 ½" x 96 ½"

Ivory Tonal
4 - 16 ½" x 42" strips, subcut into:

    49 - 2 ½" x 16 ½" rectangles   A

10 - 2 ½" x 42" strips   B

Berry Gingham
10 - 2 ¼" x 42" strips *(binding)*   C

Quilt Center

Assemble Quilt Center using the Fabric A rectangles for sashing. Press toward the sashing.

Pay close attention to the Cornerstone Block placement.

Quilt Center should measure 74 ½" x 92 ½".

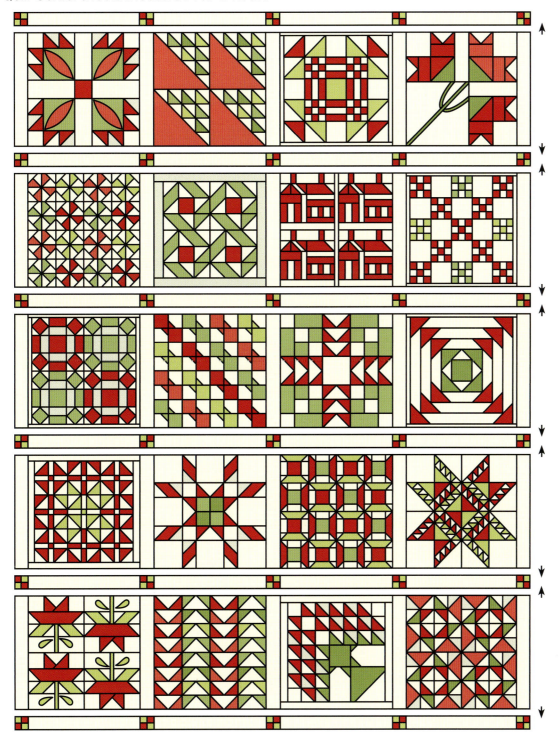

Month Twelve – Finishing

Borders

Piece the Fabric B strips end to end.

Subcut into:

      2 - 2 ½" x 92 ½" strips (Side Borders - B1)

      2 - 2 ½" x 78 ½" strips (Top and Bottom Borders - B2)

Attach the Side Borders.

Attach the Top and Bottom Borders.

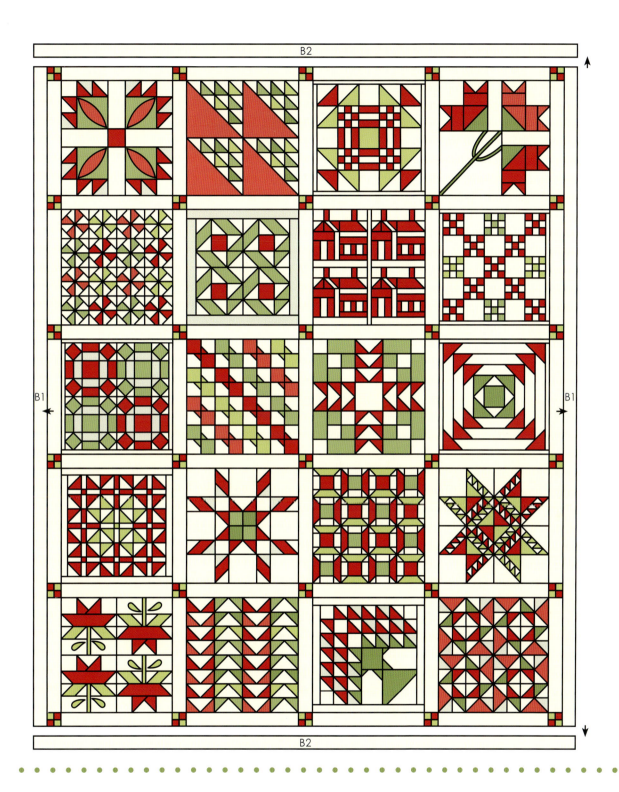

Finishing

Piece the Fabric C strips end to end for binding.

Quilt and bind as desired.

Christmas Goodies

These ten coordinating projects use the Christmas Figs Sampler Blocks and let you sprinkle the beauty of the blocks throughout your home during the holidays. You will find pillows, mini quilts, tablerunners, bedrunners, lap quilts and a lovely tree skirt to cherish. Refer to the block instructions from the Block of the Month instructions to complete the Christmas Goodies projects. This is also a wonderful opportunity to practice the skills and techniques from your favorite blocks in a new finished project!

Snowflake Stars Pillow Duo

Throw Pillow: 18 ½" x 18 ½"
Pillow Sham: 18 ½" x 28"

Sewn and quilted by: Greg Jones (@greydogwoodstudio / www.greydogwoodstudio.com)

Fabric Requirements

Yardage	Color	Description	Fabrics
⅝ yard	Ivory Tonal	Background	A, D & E
⅓ yard	Red Print	Blocks	F1 & G
⅜ yard	Red Accent Print	Blocks	F2 & H
⅜ yard	Green Print	Blocks	I, J & K
½ yard	Ivory Print	Borders	L, M & N
⅝ yard	Red Print	Binding	O & P
1 ¾ yards		Pillow Backing	Q & R
1 yard		Muslin	
Craft Size		Batting	

Cutting Instructions

Ivory Tonal (Background)

4 - 3" x 42" strips, subcut into:

  48 - 3" squares   A

4 - 1 ¼" x 42" strips, subcut into:

  52 - 1 ¼" x 2 ½" rectangles   D

  11 - 1 ¼" squares   E

Red Print (Blocks)

1 - 3" x 42" strip, subcut into:

  10 - 3" squares   F1

3 - 1 ¼" x 42" strips, subcut into:

  40 - 1 ¼" x 2 ½" rectangles   G

Red Accent Print (Blocks)

2 - 3" x 42" strips, subcut into:

  20 - 3" squares   F2

1 - 1 ¼" x 42" strip, subcut into:

  10 - 1 ¼" squares   H

Green Print (Blocks)

2 - 3" x 42" strips, subcut into:

  18 - 3" squares   I

1 - 1 ¼" x 42" strip, subcut into:

  3 - 1 ¼" squares   J

  4 - 1 ¼" x 2 ½" rectangles   K

Ivory Print (Borders)

5 - 2 ⅜" x 42" strips, subcut into:

  2 - 2 ⅜" x 28" strips   L

  2 - 2 ⅜" x 18 ½" rectangles   M

  4 - 2 ⅜" x 14 ¾" rectangles   N

Red Print (Binding)

3 - 2 ¼" x 42" strips   O

3 - 2 ¼" x 42" strips   P

Pillow Backing

1 - 33" x 42" strip, subcut into:

  2 - 19 ½" x 33" rectangles   Q

1 - 23 ½" x 42" strip, subcut into:

  2 - 19 ½" x 23 ½" rectangles   R

Muslin

1 - 29" x 42" strip, subcut into:

  1 - 19 ½" x 29" rectangle

  1 - 19 ½" square

Batting

1 - 19 ½" x 29" rectangle

1 - 19 ½" square

Refer to pages 6 to 7 for block instructions.

Puzzle Star Units

Corner Unit should measure 5 ¼" x 5 ¼".

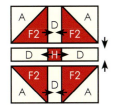 

Throw Pillow: Make four.

Pillow Sham: Make six.

Middle Unit should measure 5 ¼" x 5 ¼".

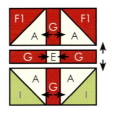 

Throw Pillow: Make four.

Pillow Sham: Make six.

Snowflake Stars Pillow Duo

Center Unit should measure 5 ¼" x 5 ¼".

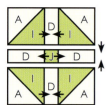 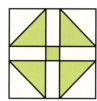

Throw Pillow: Make one.

Pillow Sham: Make two.

Assemble Unit.

Alternative Center Unit should measure 5 ¼" x 5 ¼".

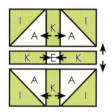 

Throw Pillow: Make zero.

Pillow Sham: Make one.

Throw Pillow Center

Assemble Throw Pillow Center.

Throw Pillow Center should measure 14 ¾" x 14 ¾".

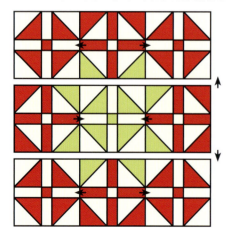

Make one.

Throw Pillow Borders

Attach side borders using the Fabric N rectangles.

Attach top and bottom borders using the Fabric M rectangles.

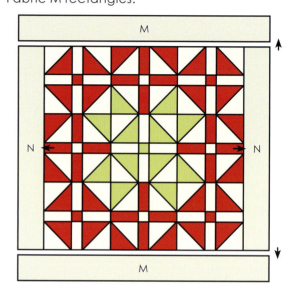

Quilted Throw Pillow Top

Layer the Throw Pillow Top, the 19 ½" Batting square and the 19 ½" Muslin square.

Quilt as desired. Trim excess Batting and Muslin.

Baste ⅛" around the inside of the Quilted Throw Pillow Top.

Quilted Throw Pillow Top will shrink after quilting.

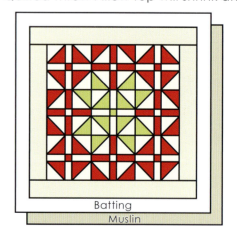

Throw Pillow Back

With wrong sides facing, fold a Fabric R rectangle in half.

Partial Throw Pillow Back should measure 11 ¾" x 19 ½".

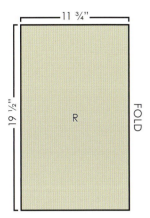

Make two.

Layer two Partial Throw Pillow Backs and overlap them 4" with folds in the center and raw edges on the outside.

Pin in place.

Throw Pillow Back should measure 19 ½" x 19 ½".

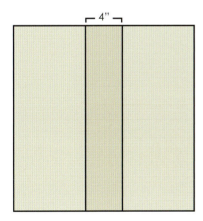

Make one.

Throw Pillow Finishing

Layer the Quilted Throw Pillow Top right side up on the Throw Pillow Back.

Trim Throw Pillow Back to the edge of the Quilted Throw Pillow Top.

Baste ⅛" around the edges.

Piece the Fabric P strips end to end for binding.

Bind as desired.

Snowflake Stars Pillow Duo

Pillow Sham Center

Assemble Pillow Sham Center.

Pillow Sham Center should measure 14 ¾" x 24 ¼".

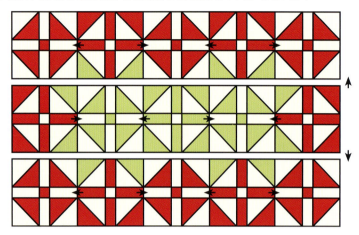

Pillow Sham Borders

Attach side borders using the Fabric N rectangles.

Attach top and bottom borders using the Fabric L strips.

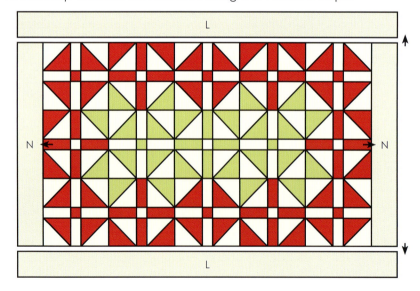

Quilted Pillow Sham Top

Layer the Pillow Sham Top, the 19 ½" x 29" Batting rectangle and the 19 ½" x 29" Muslin rectangle.

Quilt as desired. Trim excess Batting and Muslin.

Baste ⅛" around the inside of the Quilted Pillow Sham Top.

Quilted Pillow Sham Top will shrink after quilting.

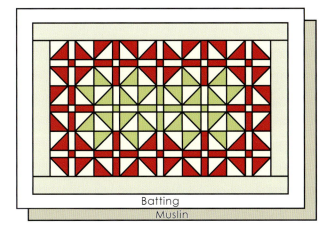

Batting
Muslin

Pillow Sham Back

With wrong sides facing, fold a Fabric Q rectangle in half.

Partial Pillow Sham Back should measure 16 ½" x 19 ½".

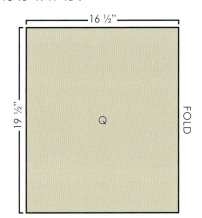

16 ½"

19 ½"

Q

FOLD

Make two.

Layer two Partial Pillow Sham Backs and overlap them 4" with folds in the center and raw edges on the outside.

Pin in place.

Pillow Sham Back should measure 19 ½" x 29".

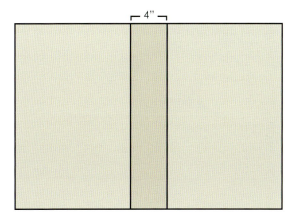

4"

Make one.

Pillow Sham Finishing

Layer the Quilted Pillow Sham Top right side up on the Pillow Sham Back.

Trim Pillow Sham Back to the edge of the Quilted Pillow Sham Top.

Baste ⅛" around the edges.

Piece the Fabric O strips end to end for binding.

Bind as desired.

Once Upon a Midnight Star Mini

20 ½" x 20 ½"

Sewn by: Cynthia Bird (@cynthia.bird) • Quilted by: Diana Johnson (@quiltedgrammy)

Fabric Requirements

Yardage	Color	Description	Fabrics
⅝ yard	Ivory Tonal	Background and Borders	A, C, D, K & L
10" x 15"	Ivory Print	Block	B
Fat Quarter	Red Print	Block	E, F & G
Fat Quarter	Green Print	Block	H, I & J
⅓ yard	Red Print	Binding	M
⅞ yard		Backing	

Cutting Instructions

Ivory Tonal (Background)	
1 - 5" x 42" strip, subcut into:	
4 - 5" squares	A
2 - 3" x 42" strips, subcut into:	
3 - 3" squares	C
From remainder of strips cut:	
24 - 2 ¼" squares	D
Ivory Print (Block)	
2 - 4 ½" x 15" strips, subcut into:	
4 - 4 ½" squares	B
Red Print (Block)	
1 - 3 ½" x 21" strip, subcut into:	
4 - 3 ½" squares	E
1 - 3" x 21" strip, subcut into:	
3 - 3" squares	F
2 - 2 ¼" x 21" strips, subcut into:	
12 - 2 ¼" squares	G
Green Print (Block)	
1 - 3 ½" x 21" strip, subcut into:	
4 - 3 ½" squares	H
1 - 3" x 21" strip, subcut into:	
3 - 3" squares	I
2 - 2 ¼" x 21" strips, subcut into:	
12 - 2 ¼" squares	J
Ivory Tonal (Borders)	
2 - 2 ½" x 42" strips, subcut into:	
2 - 2 ½" x 20 ½" strips	K
2 - 2 ½" x 16 ½" rectangles	L
Red Print (Binding)	
3 - 2 ¼" x 42" strips	M

Refer to pages 16 to 19 for block instructions.

Feather Star Block

Feather Star Block should measure 16 ½" x 16 ½".

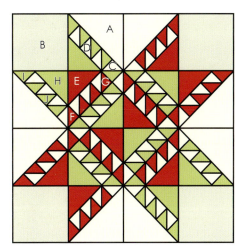

Make one.

Borders

Attach side borders using the Fabric L rectangles.

Attach top and bottom borders using the Fabric K strips.

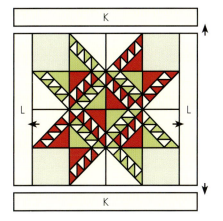

Finishing

Piece the Fabric M strips end to end for binding.

Quilt and bind as desired.

Nine Patch Sparkle Tree Skirt

55 ½" x 55 ½"

Sewn by: Sherri McConnell (@aquiltinglife / www.aquiltinglife.com) • Quilted by: Marion Bott

Fabric Requirements

Yardage	Color	Description	Fabrics
1 ¼ yards	Ivory Tonal	Background	A & B
Six ⅓ yards	Ivory Prints	Blocks	E
Four Fat Quarters	Red Prints	Blocks	F & G
Four Fat Quarters	Green Prints	Blocks	H & I
1 ⅛ yards	Ivory Print	Borders	J
⅞ yard	Red Print	Binding	K
3 ⅔ yards		Backing	

Cutting Instructions

Ivory Tonal (Background)	
24 - 1 ½" x 42" strips, subcut into:	
24 - 1 ½" x 21" strips	A
24 - 1 ½" x 21" strips	B
From each Ivory Print (Blocks)	
2 - 3 ½" x 42" strips, subcut into:	
19 - 3 ½" squares	E
From each Red Print (Blocks)	
8 - 1 ½" x 21" strips	F
2 - 1 ½" x 21" strips	G
From each Green Print (Blocks)	
4 - 1 ½" x 21" strips	H
1 - 1 ½" x 21" strip	I
Ivory Print (Borders)	
6 - 5 ½" x 42" strips	J
Red Print (Binding)	
11 - 2 ¼" x 42" strips	K

Refer to pages 20 to 23 for block instructions.

Nine Patchwork Blocks

To make the Red Nine Patch Units you need:

- Four Red Outside Strip Sets from each Red Print
- Forty Red Outside Nine Patch Units from each Red Print
- Two Red Inside Strip Sets from each Red Print
- Twenty Red Inside Nine Patch Units from each Red Print

Red Nine Patch Unit should measure 3 ½" x 3 ½".

Make twenty from each red print.

Make eighty total.

To make the Green Nine Patch Units you need:

- Two Green Outside Strip Sets from each Green Print
- Sixteen Green Outside Nine Patch Units from each Green Print
- One Green Inside Strip Set from each Green Print
- Eight Green Inside Nine Patch Units from each Green Print

Green Nine Patch Unit should measure 3 ½" x 3 ½".

Make eight from each green print.

Make thirty-two total.

Nine Patch Sparkle Tree Skirt

Assemble Block. Unit placement is intended to be scrappy.

Nine Patchwork Block One should measure 15 ½" x 15 ½".

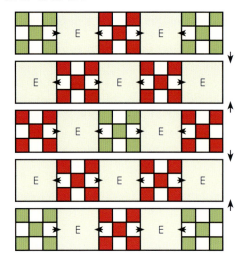

Make two.

Assemble Block. Unit placement is intended to be scrappy.

Nine Patchwork Block Two should measure 15 ½" x 15 ½".

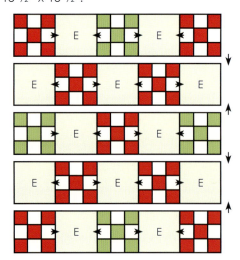

Make two.

Assemble Block. Unit placement is intended to be scrappy.

Nine Patchwork Block Three should measure 15 ½" x 15 ½".

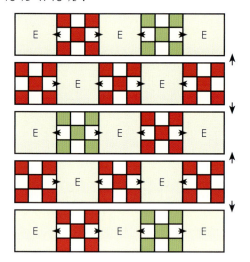

Make four.

Assemble Block. Unit placement is intended to be scrappy.

Nine Patchwork Block Four should measure 15 ½" x 15 ½".

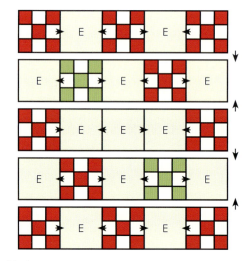

Make one.

You will not use one Fabric E square.

Tree Skirt Center

Assemble Tree Skirt Center. Pay close attention to block placement.

Tree Skirt Center should measure 45 ½" x 45 ½".

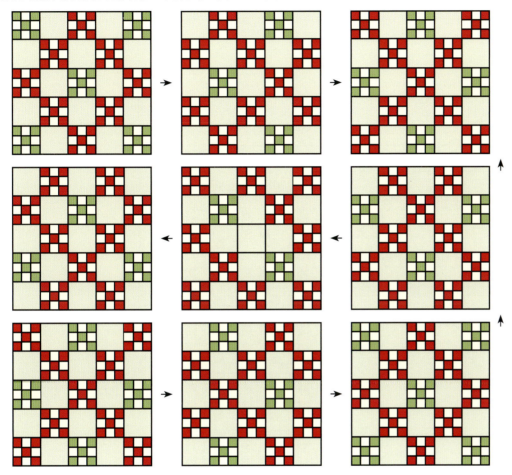

Nine Patch Sparkle Tree Skirt

Borders

Piece the Fabric J strips end to end.

Subcut into:

      2 - 5 ½" x 45 ½" strips (Side Borders - J1)

      2 - 5 ½" x 55 ½" strips (Top and Bottom Borders - J2)

Attach the Side Borders.

Attach the Top and Bottom Borders.

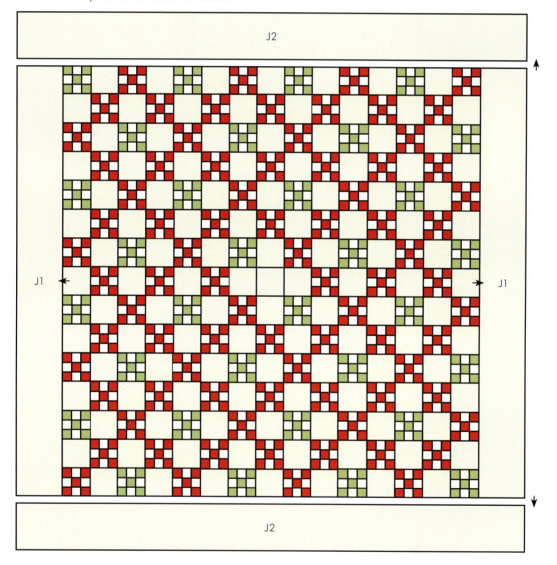

Finishing

Quilt as desired.

Using the diagram below for placement, place a 7 ½" square ruler in the center of the tree skirt. Mark the Center Square.

Cut the Center Square and the Tree Skirt Opening following the diagram below for placement.

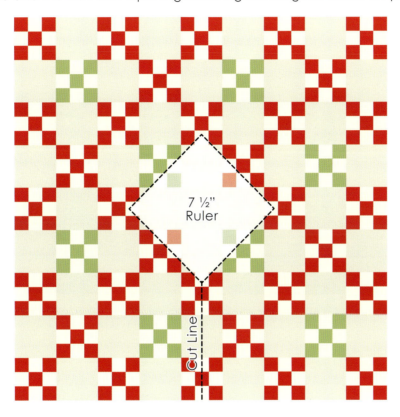

Piece the Fabric K strips end to end for binding.

You will need approximately 275" of binding for the Tree Skirt Opening and outside of the Tree Skirt.

Bind the Tree Skirt Opening and the outside of the Tree Skirt leaving the Center Square unbound.

You will need approximately 100" of binding for the Center Square and ties.

Leave a 20" tail on each end of the remaining binding and bind Center Square.

Fold raw ends of ties under and finish stitching for ties.

Poinsettia Trio Tabletopper

41 ½" x 41 ½"

Sewn by: Carrie Nelson (@justcarrieintexas / blog.modafabrics.com) • Quilted by: Carrie Straka (@redvelvet_quilts)

Fabric Requirements

Yardage	Color	Description	Fabrics
1 ⅓ yards	Ivory Print	Background	A to D
⅝ yard	Red Print	Blocks	E, F & G
Fat Quarter	Red Accent Print	Blocks	E, F & G
1 yard	Green Print	Blocks	H & I
1 yard	Ivory Tonal	Sashing and Cornerstones	J to M
Fat Quarter	Red Print	Sashing and Cornerstones	N, O & P
½ yard	Green Print	Binding	Q
2 ⅞ yards		Backing	

Cutting Instructions

Ivory Print (Background)

2 - 10 ½" x 42" strips, subcut into:
    4 - 10 ½" squares   A

2 - 4" x 42" strips, subcut into:
    12 - 4" squares   B

2 - 2 ½" x 42" strips, subcut into:
    8 - 2 ½" x 7 ½" rectangles   C

3 - 2 ¼" x 42" strips, subcut into:
    24 - 2 ¼" x 4" rectangles   D

Red Print (Blocks)

2 - 4 ½" x 42" strips, subcut into:
    4 - 4 ½" squares   E
    From remainder of strips cut:
    16 - 2 ¼" x 4" rectangles   F

2 - 2 ¼" x 42" strips, subcut into:
    32 - 2 ¼" squares   G

Red Accent Print (Blocks)

1 - 4 ½" x 21" strip, subcut into:
    2 - 4 ½" squares   E

4 - 2 ¼" x 21" strips, subcut into:
    8 - 2 ¼" x 4" rectangles   F
    16 - 2 ¼" squares   G

Green Print (Blocks)

2 - 12" x 42" strips, subcut into:
    4 - 12" squares   H

1 - 4 ½" x 42" strip, subcut into:
    6 - 4 ½" squares   I

Ivory Tonal (Sashing and Cornerstones)

1 - 4 ½" x 42" strip, subcut into:
    4 - 4 ½" squares   J

6 - 3 ½" x 42" strips, subcut into:
    8 - 3 ½" x 16 ½" rectangles   K
    4 - 3 ½" x 15" rectangles   L

1 - 2" x 42" strip, subcut into:
    8 - 2" squares   M

Red Print (Sashing and Cornerstones)

1 - 4 ½" x 21" strip, subcut into:
    4 - 4 ½" squares   N

1 - 3 ½" x 21" strip, subcut into:
    1 - 3 ½" square   O
    4 - 2" x 3 ½" rectangles   P

Green Print (Binding)

5 - 2 ¼" x 42" strips   Q

½" Bias Tape Maker

Applique Glue

Poinsettia Trio Tabletopper

Refer to pages 26 to 29 for block instructions.

Lily Trio Blocks

Lily Trio Block should measure 16 ½" x 16 ½".

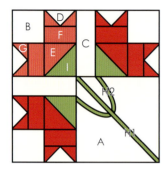

Make four.

Sashing Blocks

Draw a diagonal line on the wrong side of the Fabric M squares.

With right sides facing, layer a Fabric M square on one end of a Fabric P rectangle.

Stitch on the drawn line and trim ¼" away from the seam.

Repeat on the opposite end.

Flying Geese Unit should measure 2" x 3 ½".

Make four.

Assemble Block.

Sashing Block should measure 3 ½" x 16 ½".

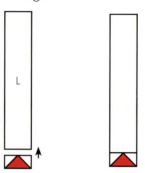

Make four.

Cornerstone Blocks

Cut on the diagonal twice.

Make sixteen.

Make sixteen.

Assemble Block.

Trim Cornerstone Block to measure 3 ½" x 3 ½".

Make eight.

Tabletopper Center

Assemble Tabletopper Center. Press toward the sashing.

Tabletopper Center should measure 41 ½" x 41 ½".

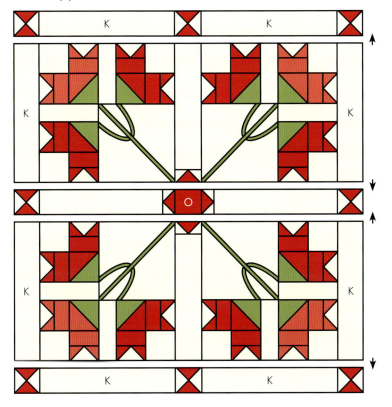

Finishing

Piece the Fabric Q strips end to end for binding.

Quilt and bind as desired.

Christmas Tree Farm Bedrunner

20 ½" x 80 ½"

Sewn by: Cheryl Hadley (@cahslz) • Quilted by: Marion Bott

Fabric Requirements

Yardage	Color	Description	Fabrics
⅔ yard	Ivory Tonal	Background and Sashing	A, B & O
⅜ yard	Ivory Print	Blocks	C
Four Fat Eighths	Ivory Accent Prints	Blocks	D
⅝ yard	Ivory Print	Background	E, F & G
Four Fat Quarters	Red Prints	Blocks	H
⅝ yard	Green Print	Blocks	I to M
Eight 10" squares	Ivory Prints	Sashing	N
⅝ yard	Ivory Print	Borders	P & Q
⅝ yard	Red Print	Binding	R
2 ½ yards		Backing	

Cutting Instructions

Ivory Tonal (Background)
8 - 1 ½" x 42" strips, subcut into:
 8 - 1 ½" x 16 ½" rectangles A
 8 - 1 ½" x 14 ½" rectangles B

Ivory Print (Blocks)
3 - 3" x 42" strips, subcut into:
 32 - 3" squares C

From each Ivory Accent Print (Blocks)
1 - 3" x 21" strip, subcut into:
 6 - 3" squares D

Ivory Print (Background)
1 - 5 ½" x 42" strip, subcut into:
 8 - 3 ½" x 5 ½" rectangles E

1 - 5" x 42" strip, subcut into:
 4 - 5" squares F

2 - 2 ½" x 42" strips, subcut into:
 20 - 2 ½" squares G

From each Red Print (Blocks)
2 - 3" x 21" strips, subcut into:
 10 - 3" squares H

Green Print (Blocks)
1 - 5 ½" x 42" strip, subcut into:
 4 - 5 ½" squares I
 From remainder of strip cut:
 4 - 3 ½" squares J

2 - 3" x 42" strips, subcut into:
 16 - 3" squares K

1 - 2" x 42" strip, subcut into:
 8 - 2" squares L

1 - 1 ½" x 42" strip, subcut into:
 8 - 1 ½" squares M

From each Ivory Print (Sashing)
1 - 3" x 10" strip, subcut into:
 3 - 3" squares N

Ivory Tonal (Sashing)
2 - 3" x 42" strips, subcut into:
 24 - 3" squares O

Ivory Print (Borders)
5 - 2 ½" x 42" strips P

1 - 2 ½" x 42" strip, subcut into:
 2 - 2 ½" x 16 ½" rectangles Q

Red Print (Binding)
6 - 2 ¼" x 42" strips R

Christmas Tree Farm Bedrunner

Refer to pages 34 to 37 for block instructions.

Tree of Life Blocks

Pair a Fabric D square with a Fabric H square for the Tree of Life Blocks (pair).

Tree of Life Block should measure 16 ½" x 16 ½".

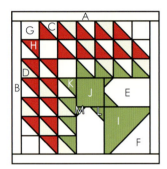

Make one from each pair.

Make four total.

Sashing Blocks

Cut on the diagonal once.

Make forty-eight.

Make six from each ivory print.

Make forty-eight total.

Assemble Unit.

Trim Sashing Half Square Triangle Unit to measure 2 ½" x 2 ½".

Make six from each ivory print.

Make forty-eight total.

Assemble Unit using different fabrics.

Pinwheel Unit should measure 4 ½" x 4 ½".

Make twelve.

Assemble Block.

Sashing Block should measure 4 ½" x 16 ½".

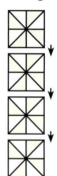 

Make three.

Christmas Figs by Joanna Figueroa of Fig Tree & Co.

Bedrunner Center

Assemble Bedrunner Center.

Bedrunner Center should measure 16 ½" x 76 ½".

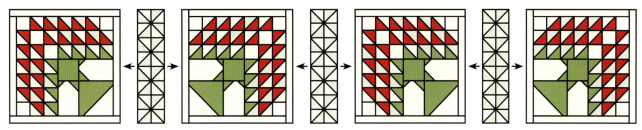

Borders

Piece the Fabric P strips end to end.

Subcut into:

      2 - 2 ½ x 80 ½" strips (Top and Bottom Borders)

Attach side borders using the Fabric Q rectangles.

Attach the Top and Bottom Borders.

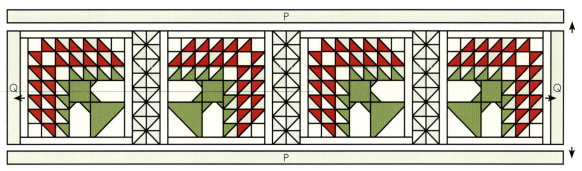

Finishing

Piece the Fabric R strips end to end for binding.

Quilt and bind as desired.

Candy Cane Patchwork Tablerunner

21 ½" x 63 ½"

Sewn by: Susan Vaughan (@thefeltedpear) • Quilted by: Lorna Cronk (@leavenoscrapbehind)

Fabric Requirements

Yardage	Color	Description	Fabrics
1 ¼ yards	Ivory Tonal	Background, Sashing and Borders	A & J
⅝ yard	Ivory Print	Blocks	D & E
½ yard	Red Print	Blocks	F & G
⅜ yard	Green Print	Blocks	H & I
Ten Fat Quarters	Ivory Prints	Sashing and Borders	K & L
½ yard	Red Print	Binding	M
2 yards		Backing	

Cutting Instructions

Ivory Tonal (Background and Borders)	
20 - 1 ½" x 42" strips, subcut into:	
39 - 1 ½" x 21" strips	A
Ivory Print (Blocks)	
2 - 4" x 42" strips, subcut into:	
18 - 4" squares	D
2 - 3 ½" x 42" strips, subcut into:	
12 - 3 ½" squares	E
Red Print (Blocks)	
1 - 4" x 42" strip, subcut into:	
6 - 4" squares	F
5 - 1 ½" x 42" strips, subcut into:	
9 - 1 ½" x 21" strips	G
Green Print (Blocks)	
2 - 4" x 42" strips, subcut into:	
12 - 4" squares	H
From remainder of strip cut:	
3 - 3 ½" squares	I
Ivory Tonal (Sashing)	
2 - 3 ½" x 42" strips, subcut into:	
10 - 3 ½" x 6 ½" rectangles	J
From each Ivory Print (Sashing and Borders)	
1 - 3 ½" x 21" strip, subcut into:	
2 - 3 ½" squares	K
3 - 1 ½" x 21" strips	L
Red Print (Binding)	
5 - 2 ¼" x 42" strips	M

Refer to pages 40 to 43 for block instructions.

Goose in the Pond Blocks

To make the Goose in the Pond Blocks you need:

- Three Ivory Strip Sets
- Twenty-four Ivory Nine Patch Units
- Three Red Strip Sets
- Twelve Rail Fence Units
- Twelve Red Nine Patch Units

Goose in the Pond Block should measure 15 ½" x 15 ½".

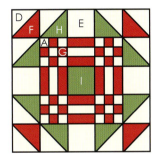

Make three.

Sashing Blocks

Draw a diagonal line on the wrong side of the Fabric K squares.

With right sides facing, layer a Fabric K square on one end of a Fabric J rectangle.

Stitch on the drawn line and trim ¼" away from the seam.

Repeat on the opposite end with a matching Fabric K square.

Flying Geese Unit should measure 3 ½" x 6 ½".

Make one from each ivory print.

Make ten total.

Candy Cane Patchwork Tablerunner

Assemble Block.

Sashing Block should measure 6 ½" x 15 ½".

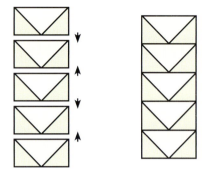

Make two.

Tablerunner Center

Assemble Tablerunner Center.

Tablerunner Center should measure 15 ½" x 57 ½".

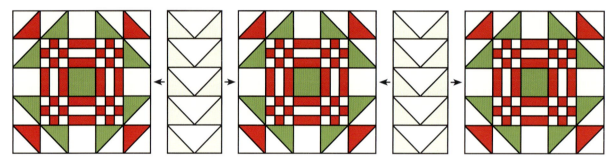

Borders

Assemble two matching Fabric L strips and one Fabric A strip.

Ivory Print Strip Set should measure 3 ½" x 21".

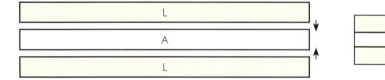

Make one from each ivory print.

Make ten total.

Subcut each Ivory Print Strip Set into nine 1 ½" x 3 ½" rectangles.

Ivory Print Nine Patch Unit should measure 1 ½" x 3 ½".

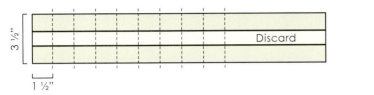

Make nine from each ivory print.

Make ninety total.

Assemble two Fabric A strips and one Fabric L strip.

Ivory Tonal Strip Set should measure 3 ½" x 21".

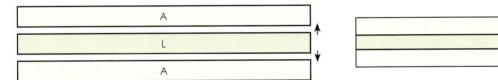

Make one from each ivory print.

Make ten total.

Subcut each Ivory Tonal Strip Set into nine 1 ½" x 3 ½" rectangles.

Ivory Tonal Nine Patch Unit should measure 1 ½" x 3 ½".

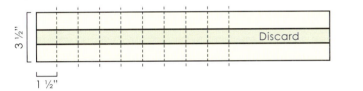

Make nine from each ivory print.

Make ninety total.

Assemble Unit using matching fabric.

Ivory Print Nine Patch Unit should measure 3 ½" x 3 ½".

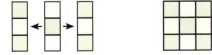

Make three from each ivory print.

Make thirty total.

Candy Cane Patchwork Tablerunner

Assemble Unit using matching fabric.

Ivory Tonal Nine Patch Unit should measure 3 ½" x 3 ½".

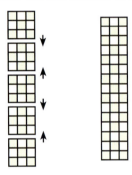

Make three from each ivory print.

Make thirty total.

Assemble Side Border.

Side Border should measure 3 ½" x 15 ½".

Make two.

Assemble Top and Bottom Border.

Top and Bottom Border should measure 3 ½" x 63 ½".

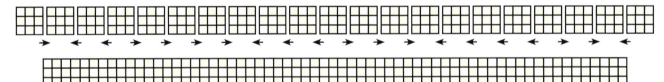

Make two.

You will not use all Nine Patch Units.

Attach the Side Borders.

Attach the Top and Bottom Borders.

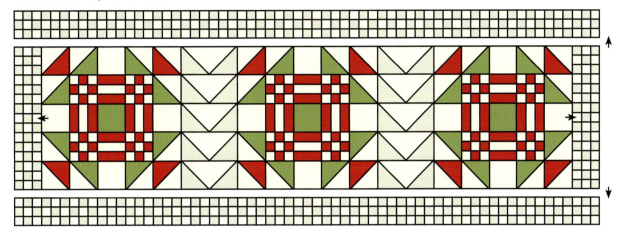

Finishing

Piece the Fabric M strips end to end for binding.

Quilt and bind as desired.

Christmas Lilies Wallhanging

32 ½" x 32 ½"

Sewn by: Taunja Kelvington (@taunjalynn / www.CarriedAwayQuilting.com) • Quilted by: Barb Erickson

Fabric Requirements

Yardage	Color	Description	Fabrics
1 ½ yards	Ivory Tonal	Background, Sashing and Borders	A to D & J to N
Three Fat Quarters	Red Prints	Blocks	E & F
Three Fat Quarters	Green Prints	Blocks	G, H & I
Nine 10" squares	Ivory Prints	Borders	O
⅜ yard	Red Print	Binding	P
1 ⅛ yards		Backing	

Cutting Instructions

Ivory Tonal (Background)

3 - 3¾" x 42" strips, subcut into:
- 18 - 3¾" x 5¼" rectangles — A

3 - 2¾" x 42" strips, subcut into:
- 9 - 2¾" x 4" rectangles — B
- 18 - 2¾" squares — C

4 - 2¼" x 42" strips, subcut into:
- 54 - 2¼" squares — D

From each Red Print (Blocks)

1 - 2¾" x 21" strip, subcut into:
- 6 - 2¾" squares — E

2 - 2¼" x 21" strips, subcut into:
- 3 - 2¼" x 8½" rectangles — F

From each Green Print (Blocks)

1 - 3" x 21" strip
- 6 - applique pieces — G

2 - 2¼" x 21" strips, subcut into:
- 6 - 2¼" x 4¼" rectangles — H

1 - 1" x 21" strip, subcut into:
- 3 - 1" x 4½" rectangles — I

Ivory Tonal (Sashing and Borders)

8 - 1" x 42" strips, subcut into:
- 6 - 1" x 8½" rectangles — J
- 2 - 1" x 26½" strips — K
- 4 - 1" x 25½" strips — L

4 - 2½" x 42" strips, subcut into:
- 2 - 2½" x 32½" strips — M
- 2 - 2½" x 28½" strips — N

From each Ivory Print (Borders)

2 - 1½" x 10" strips, subcut into:
- 12 - 1½" squares — O

Red Print (Binding)

4 - 2¼" x 42" strips — P

Refer to pages 44 to 47 for block instructions.

Carolina Lily Blocks

Pair a Red Print with a Green Print for the Carolina Lily Blocks (pair).

Carolina Lily Block should measure 8½" x 8½".

Make three from each pair.

Make nine total.

Quilt Rows

Assemble Quilt Row using matching Blocks.

Quilt Row should measure 8½" x 25½".

Make one from each pair.

Make three total.

Christmas Lilies Wallhanging

Wallhanging Center

Assemble Wallhanging Center.

Wallhanging Center should measure 25 ½" x 25 ½".

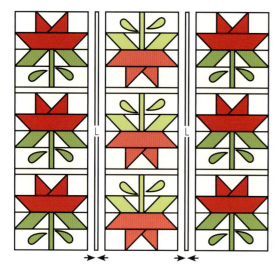

Borders

Attach side inner borders using the Fabric L strips.

Attach top and bottom inner borders using the Fabric K strips.

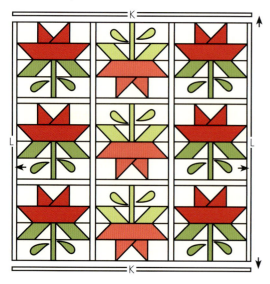

Assemble twenty-six Fabric O squares.

Side Middle Border should measure 1 ½" x 26 ½".

Make two.

Assemble twenty-eight Fabric O squares.

Top and Bottom Middle Border should measure 1 ½" x 28 ½".

Make two.

Attach the Side Middle Borders.

Attach the Top and Bottom Middle Borders.

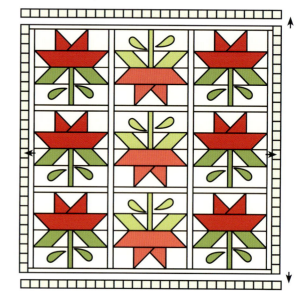

Attach side outer borders using the Fabric N strips.

Attach top and bottom outer borders using the Fabric M strips.

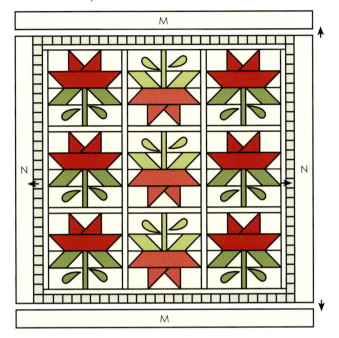

Finishing

Piece the Fabric P strips end to end for binding.

Quilt and bind as desired.

Holiday Homespun Quilt

48 ½" x 64 ½"

Sewn and quilted by: Diana Johnson (@quiltedgrammy)

Fabric Requirements

Yardage	Color	Description	Fabrics
Eight ⅝ yards	Ivory Prints	Blocks	A
Four ⅝ yards	Red Prints	Blocks	B
Four ⅝ yards	Green Prints	Blocks	C
⅝ yard	Red Print	Binding	D
3 ¼ yards		Backing	

Cutting Instructions

From each Ivory Print (Blocks)	
6 - 2 ½" x 42" strips, subcut into:	
48 - 2 ½" x 4 ½" rectangles	A
From each Red Print (Blocks)	
6 - 2 ½" x 42" strips, subcut into:	
96 - 2 ½" squares	B
From each Green Print (Blocks)	
6 - 2 ½" x 42" strips, subcut into:	
96 - 2 ½" squares	C
Red Print (Binding)	
7 - 2 ¼" x 42" strips	D

Refer to pages 50 to 51 for block instructions.

Flying Geese Blocks

Fabric placement is intended to be scrappy.

Flying Geese Block should measure 16 ½" x 16 ½".

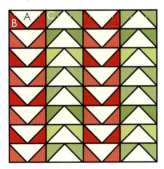

Make twelve.

Quilt Center

Assemble Quilt Center. Press rows in opposite directions.

Quilt Center should measure 48 ½" x 64 ½".

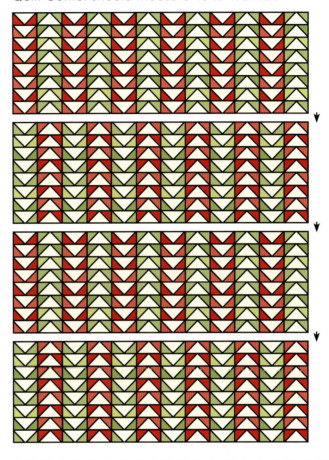

Finishing

Piece the Fabric D strips end to end for binding.

Quilt and bind as desired.

Peppermints & Cream Quilt

58 ½" x 66 ½"

Sewn by: Susan Ache (@yardgrl60) • Quilted by: Susan Rogers

Fabric Requirements

Yardage	Color	Description	Fabrics
2 yards	Ivory Tonal	Background	A
Two 1 yards	Ivory Prints	Blocks	B
Two 1 yards	Ivory Prints	Blocks	C
Four ⅝ yards	Red Prints	Blocks	D
Four ⅝ yards	Green Prints	Blocks	E
⅞ yard	Ivory Print	Borders	F
⅝ yard	Red Print	Binding	G
3 ⅞ yards		Backing	

Cutting Instructions

Ivory Tonal (Background)	
37 - 1 ¾" x 42" strips, subcut into:	
800 - 1 ¾" squares	A

From each Ivory Print (Blocks)	
9 - 3" x 42" strips, subcut into:	
100 - 3" squares	B

From each Ivory Print (Blocks)	
9 - 3" x 42" strips, subcut into:	
100 - 3" squares	C

From each Red Print (Blocks)	
5 - 3" x 42" strips, subcut into:	
50 - 3" squares	D

From each Green Print (Blocks)	
5 - 3" x 42" strips, subcut into:	
50 - 3" squares	E

Ivory Print (Borders)	
7 - 3 ½" x 42" strips	F

Red Print (Binding)	
7 - 2 ¼" x 42" strips	G

Refer to pages 54 to 57 for block instructions.

Peppermint Blocks

Red Peppermint Block should measure 4 ½" x 4 ½".

Make twenty-five from each red print.

Make one hundred total.

Green Peppermint Block should measure 4 ½" x 4 ½".

Make twenty-five from each green print.

Make one hundred total.

Christmas Figs by Joanna Figueroa of Fig Tree & Co.

Peppermints & Cream Quilt

Quilt Center

Assemble Quilt Center. Press rows in opposite directions.

Quilt Center should measure 52 ½" x 60 ½".

You will not use all Peppermint Blocks.

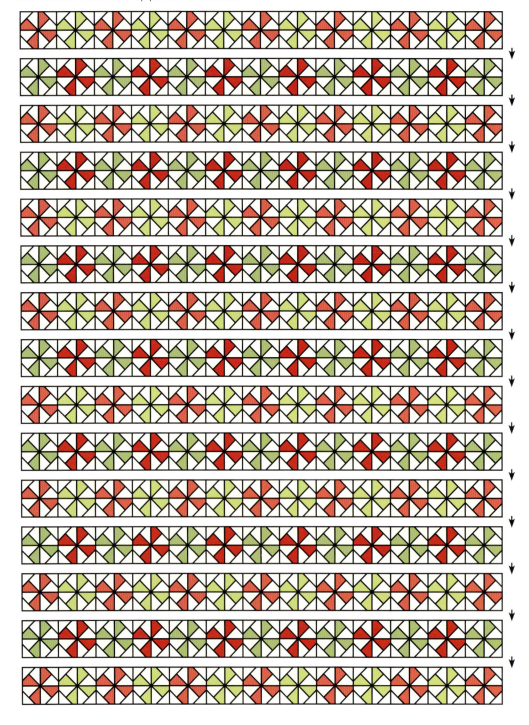

Borders

Piece the Fabric F strips end to end.

Subcut into:

      2 - 3 ½" x 60 ½" strips (Side Borders - F1)

      2 - 3 ½" x 58 ½" strips (Top and Bottom Borders - F2)

Attach the Side Borders.

Attach the Top and Bottom Borders.

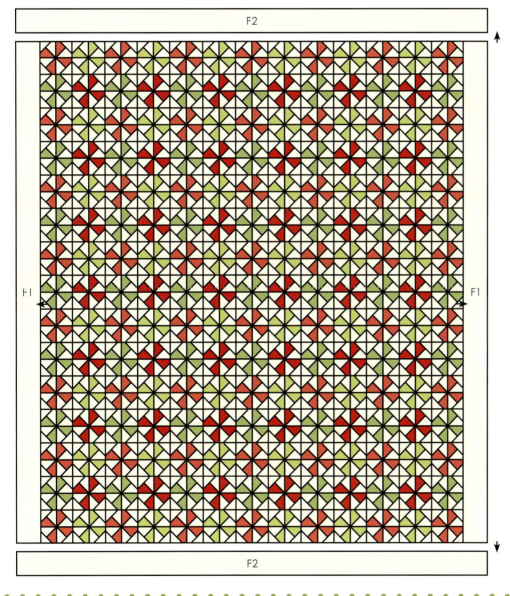

Finishing

Piece the Fabric G strips end to end for binding.

Quilt and bind as desired.

Classic Schoolhouse Pillow

20 ½" x 37"

Sewn and quilted by: Joanna Figueroa (@figtreeandco / FigTreeQuilts.typepad.com)

Fabric Requirements

Yardage	Color	Description	Fabrics
½ yard	Ivory Print	Sashing and Borders	A, S & T
Four Fat Quarters	Ivory Prints	Blocks	B to I
Two ⅜ yards	Red Prints	Blocks	J to R
⅜ yard	Red Print	Binding	U
1 ¼ yards		Backing	V
¾ yard		Muslin	
Craft Size		Batting	

Cutting Instructions

Ivory Print (Sashing)

2 - 1" x 42" strips, subcut into:

   3 - 1" x 16 ½" rectangles   A

From each Ivory Print (Blocks)

2 - 2 ½" x 21" strips, subcut into:

   1 - 2 ½" square   B

   From remainder of strips cut:

   2 - 2" x 3 ¾" rectangles   C

   2 - 2" x 2 ¾" rectangles   D

   6 - 2" squares   E

2 - 1 ½" x 21" strips, subcut into:

   2 - 1 ½" x 8 ¼" rectangles   F

   2 - 1 ½" x 3 ¼" rectangles   G

   4 - 1 ½" x 2" rectangles   H

1 - 1 ¼" x 21" strip, subcut into:

   4 - 1 ¼" x 4 ½" rectangles   I

From each Red Print (Blocks)

1 - 2 ½" x 42" strip, subcut into:

   2 - 2 ½" squares   J

   From remainder of strip cut:

   4 - 2" x 4 ½" rectangles   K

   8 - 2" squares   L

2 - 1 ¾" x 42" strips, subcut into:

   4 - 1 ¾" x 3 ½" rectangles   M

   From remainder of strips cut:

   4 - 1 ½" x 4 ½" rectangles   N

   8 - 1 ½" x 3 ¼" rectangles   O

2 - 1 ¼" x 42" strips, subcut into:

   4 - 1 ¼" x 4 ½" rectangles   P

   12 - 1 ¼" x 2" rectangles   Q

1 - 1 ⅛" x 42" strip, subcut into:

   8 - 1 ⅛" x 2" rectangles   R

Ivory Print (Borders)

4 - 2 ½" x 42" strips, subcut into:

   2 - 2 ½" x 33" strips   S

   2 - 2 ½" x 20 ½" strips   T

Red Print (Binding)

4 - 2 ¼" x 42" strips   U

Backing

2 - 21 ½" x 42" rectangles   V

Muslin

1 - 21 ½" x 42" rectangle, subcut into:

   1 - 21 ½" x 38" rectangle

Batting

1 - 21 ½" x 38" rectangle

> **Refer to pages 60 to 63 for block instructions.**

Little Red Schoolhouse Blocks

Little Red Schoolhouse Block should measure 16 ½" x 16 ½".

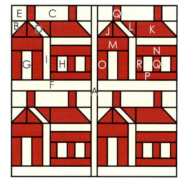

Make two.

Pillow Center

Assemble Pillow Center.

Pillow Center should measure 16 ½" x 33".

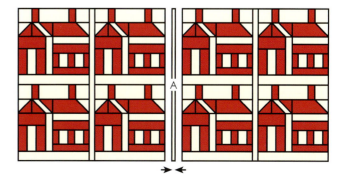

Classic Schoolhouse Pillow

Borders

Attach top and bottom borders using the Fabric S strips.

Attach side borders using the Fabric T strips.

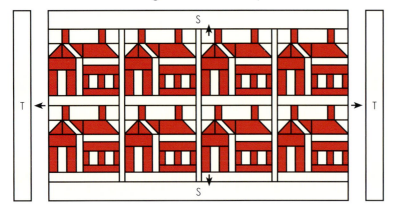

Quilted Pillow Top

Layer the Pillow Top, the Batting and the Muslin.

Quilt as desired. Trim excess Batting and Muslin.

Baste ⅛" around the inside of the Quilted Pillow Top.

Quilted Pillow Top will shrink after quilting.

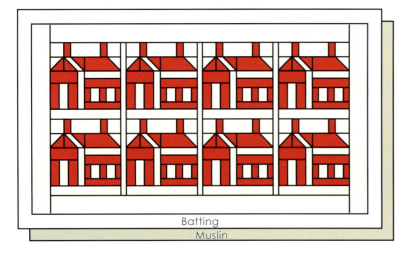

Pillow Back

With wrong sides facing, fold a Fabric V rectangle in half.

Partial Pillow Back should measure 21" x 21 ½".

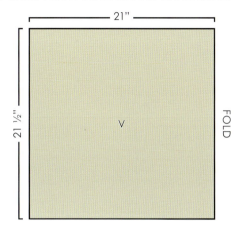

Make two.

Layer two Partial Pillow Backs and overlap them 4" with folds in the center and raw edges on the outside.

Pin in place.

Pillow Back should measure 21 ½" x 38".

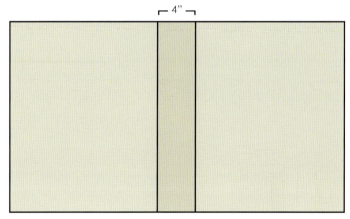

Make one.

Finishing

Layer the Quilted Pillow Top right side up on the Pillow Back.

Trim Pillow Back to the edge of the Quilted Pillow Top.

Baste ⅛" around the edges.

Piece the Fabric U strips end to end for binding.

Bind as desired.

Christmas Figs by Joanna Figueroa of Fig Tree & Co.